I0004419

THE WINNING CLUE

BY

JAMES HAY, Jr.

Author of "The Man Who Forgot," "Mrs. Marden's Ordeal," etc.

NEW YORK

DODD, MEAD AND COMPANY

1919

TO

GRAHAM B. NICHOL

AS A LITTLE TOKEN OF MY ADMIRATION
AND AFFECTION

CONTENTS

THE WINNING CLUE

CHAPTER I

STRANGLED

WHEN a woman's voice, pitched to the high note of utter terror, rang out on the late morning quiet of Manniston Road, Lawrence Bristow looked up from his newspaper quickly but vaguely, as if he doubted his own ears. He was reading an account of a murder committed in Waukesha, Wisconsin, and the shrieks he had just heard fitted in so well with the paragraph then before his eyes that his imagination might have been playing him tricks. He was allowed, however, little time for speculation or doubt.

"Murder! Help!" cried the woman in a staccato sharpness that carried the length of many blocks.

Bristow sprang to his feet and started down the short flight of stairs leading from his porch to the street. Before he had taken three steps, he saw the frightened girl standing on the porch of No. 5, two doors to his left. Although he was lame, he displayed surprising agility. His left leg, two inches shorter than the right and supported by a steel brace from foot to thigh, did not prevent his being the first to reach the young woman's side.

Late as it was, half-past ten, she was not fully dressed. She wore a kimono of light, sheer material which, clutched spasmodically about her, revealed the slightness and grace of her figure. Her fair hair hung down her back in a long, thick braid.

Neighbours across the street and further up Manniston Road were out on their porches now or starting toward No. 5. All of them were women.

The girl—she was barely past twenty, he thought—stopped screaming, and, her hands pressed to her throat and cheeks, stared wildly from him toward the front door, which was standing open. He entered the living room of the one-story bungalow. A foot within the doorway, he stood stock still. On the sofa against the opposite wall he saw another woman. He knew at first glance that she was dead.

The body was in a curious position. Apparently, before death had come, the victim had been sitting on the sofa, and, in dying, her body had crumpled over from the waist toward the right, so that now the lower part of her occupied the attitude of sitting while the upper half reclined as if in the posture of natural sleep. One thing which, perhaps, added to the gruesomeness of the sight was that she had on evening dress, a gown of pale blue satin embellished in unerring taste with real old Irish lace.

Although the face had been beautiful under its crown of luxuriant black hair, it now was distorted. While the eyes were closed, the mouth was open, very wide—an ugly, repulsive gape.

He was aware that the woman in the kimono was just behind him—he could feel her hot breath against the back of his neck—and that behind her pressed the neighbours, their number augmented by the arrival of two men. He turned and faced them.

"Call a doctor—and the police, somebody, will you?" he said sharply.

"They have a telephone back there in the dining room," volunteered one of the women on the porch.

Another, a Mrs. Allen who lived in No. 6, had put her arms around the terrified girl and was forcing her into an armchair on the porch.

The others started into the living room.

"Wait a moment," cautioned Bristow. "Don't come in here yet. The police will want to find things undisturbed. It looks like murder."

They obeyed him without question. He was about forty years old, of medium height and with good shoulders, but his chest was too flat, and his face showed an unnatural flush. His mere physique was not one to force obedience from others. It was in his eyes, dark-brown and lit with a peculiar flaming intensity, that they read his right to command.

"Please go through this room to the telephone and call a doctor," he said, singling out the woman who had spoken.

His voice, a deep barytone with a pleasant note, was perfectly steady. He seemed to hold their excitement easily within bounds.

The woman he had addressed complied with his

suggestion. While she was doing so, he crossed over to the sofa and put his hand to the wrist of the murdered woman. In order to do that, he had to move a fold of the gown which partially concealed it. The flesh was cold, and he shivered slightly, readjusting the satin to exactly the fold in which he had found it.

"Too late for a doctor to help now," he threw back over his shoulder.

They watched him silently. Low moans were coming constantly from the woman in the chair on the porch.

Bristow took the telephone in his turn and called up police headquarters.

The chief of police, whom he knew, answered the call.

"Hello! Captain Greenleaf?" asked the lame man.

"Yes."

"There's been a murder at Number Five, Manniston Road. This is Lawrence Bristow, of Number Nine."

"Aw, quit your kiddin'," laughed Greenleaf. "What do you want to do, get me up there to hear another of your theories about——"

"This is no joke," snapped Bristow. "I tell you one of the women in Number Five has been murdered. Come——"

But the chief, recognizing the urgency in the summons, had left the telephone and was on his way.

As Bristow turned toward the living room, Mrs. Allen and another woman were carrying the hysterical, moaning girl from the front porch to one of the two bedrooms in the bungalow. Some of the others again started into the living room.

"Let's wait," he cautioned once more. "If we get to moving around in here we may destroy any clues that could be used later."

When they fell back a little, he joined them on the porch, standing always so that he could watch the body and see that no one changed its attitude or even approached it. His eyes studied keenly all the furniture in the room. Save for one overturned stiff-backed chair, it apparently had not been disturbed.

The doctor arrived and, waiting for no information, approached the murdered woman. As Bristow had done, he touched her wrist, and then slipped his hand beneath her corsage so that it rested above her heart. He straightened up almost immediately.

"Dead," he said to Bristow; "dead for hours."

The physician became conscious of the hysterical girl's moans, took a step toward the bedrooms and paused.

"That's right, doctor," Bristow told him. "They need you back there."

The doctor hurried out.

"That is—that was Mrs. Withers, wasn't it?" Bristow, looking at the dead body, asked of the group.

"Yes; and the other is her sister, Miss Fulton," one of them answered.

Bristow had seemed to all of them a peculiar man—too quiet and reserved—ever since he had come to No. 9 four months before. They remembered this now, when he seemed scarcely conscious of the identity of the two girls who had lived almost next door to him during all that time.

Different members of the crowd gave him information: Miss Maria Fulton, like nearly everybody else on Manniston Road, had tuberculosis, and Mrs. Withers had been living with her. They had plenty of money—not rich, perhaps, but able to have all the comforts and most of the luxuries of life. They were here in the hope that Furmville's climate would restore Miss Fulton's health.

Their coloured cook-and-maid had not come to work that morning, it seemed, and Miss Fulton, who was the younger of the two sisters, was on the "rest" cure, ordered by the doctor to stay in bed day and night. Perhaps that was why she had not discovered Mrs. Withers' body earlier in the day.

They gossiped on.

It was like a lesson in immortality—the dead body, with distorted face and twisted limbs, just inside the room; and outside, in the low-toned phrases of the awed women, swift and vivid pictures of what she, when alive, had said and done and seemed.

"Everybody liked her. If somebody had come and told me a woman living on Manniston Road had been killed, she would have been the last one I'd have thought of as the victim." "All the other beautiful women I ever knew were stupid; she wasn't." "Her husband couldn't come to Furmville very often." "Loveliest black hair I *ever* saw." "She used to be——"

Then followed quick glimpses of her life as they had seen or heard it: a dance at Maplewood Inn where she had been the undisputed belle; a novel she had liked; a big reception at the White House in Washington when, during the year of her début, the French ambassador had called her "the most beautiful American," and the newspapers had made much of it; an emerald ring she had worn; the unfailing good humour she had always shown in the tedious routine of nursing her sister—and so on, a mass of facts and impressions which were, simultaneously, a little biography of her and an unaffected appreciation of the way she had touched and coloured their lives.

Captain Greenleaf, with one of the plain-clothes men of his force, came hurrying up the steps. The crowd fell back, gave them passage, and closed in again.

"Nothing's been disturbed, captain," said Bristow.

"Were is she?" asked Greenleaf anxiously. He was not accustomed to murder cases.

He caught sight of the body on the sofa.

"God!" he said in a low tone, and turned toward the plain-clothes man:

"Come on in, Jenkins—you, too, Mr. Bristow."

The three entered the living room, and Greenleaf, with a muttered word of apology to the onlookers, closed the door in their faces.

He, too, did what Bristow had done—put his fingers on the dead woman's wrist. He was breathing rapidly, and his hand shook. Jenkins stood motionless. He also was overwhelmed by the tragedy. Besides, he was not cut out for work of this kind. In looking for illicit distillers and bootleggers, or negroes charged with theft, he was in his element, but this sort of thing was new to him. He had no idea of where to turn or what to do.

"She's dead," Bristow said to the captain. "The doctor says she has been dead a long time—hours."

"Where's the doctor?"

"Back there. Miss Fulton, the sister, is hysterical with fright."

"Who sent for the doctor?"

"I did. I asked one of the women here to telephone."

"Then I'll call the coroner."

He stepped through the open folding doors into the dining room and took down the receiver, looking, as he did so, at the body and its surroundings.

Bristow stooped down, picked up something from the floor near the sofa and dropped it into his vest pocket.

The doctor—Dr. Braley—returned as the captain hung up the telephone receiver.

"Miss Fulton is quieter now," he announced.

"Doctor," requested Greenleaf, "look at this body, will you? What caused death?"

Braley, a thin, quick-moving little man of thirty-five, bent over the dead woman, lifted one of her eyelids, and examined her throat as far as was possible without moving the head.

"She was choked to death," he gave his opinion. "Although the eyes are closed, you see the effect they produce of almost starting from their sockets. And the tongue protrudes. Besides, there are the marks on her throat. You can see them there on the left side."

"How long has she been dead?"

"I can't say definitely. I should guess about eight or ten hours anyway."

That staggered Greenleaf, the idea of this woman dead here in the front room of a bungalow on Manniston Road for eight or ten hours—and nobody knew anything about it! His agitation grew. He felt the need of doing something, starting something.

"How about Miss Fulton?" he asked. "Can I get a statement from her?"

"Not just yet. Give her a little more time to get herself together. Besides, she told me something about the—er—affair. Most remarkable statement—most remarkable."

"What was it?"

"She says," related Braley, "that she only discovered the dead body of her sister a few minutes before she was heard crying for help. Her sister, Mrs. Withers, went to a dance, one of the regular Monday night dances at the inn—Maplewood Inn. She went with Mr. Campbell, Douglas Campbell, the real estate man here. You know him. They left the house at nine o'clock last night. That was the last time Miss Fulton saw Mrs. Withers alive.

"In the meantime, Miss Fulton herself, who is under my orders to stay in bed all the time, was up and dressed so that she might spend the evening with a friend of hers from Washington. His name is Henry Morley. He left this house a little after eleven o'clock, and he left Furmville on the midnight train for Washington.

"Miss Fulton, thoroughly tired out, went to bed and was asleep by half-past eleven. As she has something which she uses when she wants a good sleep, she took some of it last night and did not wake up until after ten this morning. She didn't even hear her sister come in last night.

"When she awoke this morning, she called her sister. Amazed by receiving no answer, she got up to investigate. Mrs. Withers' bed had not been occupied. She then came in here and found the body."

"You mean to say," put in Bristow, "that this sick girl was here all night and heard nothing?"

"That's what she says," confirmed the physician.

"Did she give any idea who the murderer might be?" queried Greenleaf.

"No; she's not sufficiently clear in her mind to advance any theories yet—naturally."

"Let me look around," suggested the captain.

He did so, followed by Bristow and the doctor. Save for the overturned chair, between the sofa and the dining room door, the furniture, for the most part the mission stuff generally found in the furnished-for-rent cottages in Furmville, had not been knocked about in a struggle. That was evident. The two rugs on the floor had not been disturbed. None of the three men touched the overturned chair.

All the windows of the living room and the dining

room were closed but not locked, as there was on the outside of each the usual covering of mosquito wiring. The shades were down. The front door did not have the inside "catch" thrown on.

Greenleaf examined the kitchen, the unoccupied bedroom, the bathroom, and the sleeping porch at the back of the house. This last, like the windows, was inclosed in stout wire screens, and nowhere, on either the windows or the sleeping porch, had this screening been broken. The kitchen door was locked. There was no sign of a struggle anywhere. These negative facts were gathered quickly.

Mrs. Allen, summoned from the sister's side, reported that there were no signs of an entrance having been made through any of the three windows in the bedroom in which Miss Fulton now lay quiet.

They made their way back to the living room. In spite of the most painstaking examination of the floor, walls, and furniture of the entire bungalow, they were, so far, without a clue. The murderer had left not the slightest trace of his identity or his manner of entrance to the death chamber.

"As I see it," said the captain when they rejoined Jenkins, "nobody broke into this house last night. But two men had admission to it. They were Mr. Douglas Campbell, the real estate man, and Mr. Henry Morley, who was calling on Miss Fulton. It's up to those two to tell what they know."

"But," objected the doctor, "Miss Fulton says Morley left town last night."

"Humph! Maybe that makes it look all the worse for Morley."

"But," suggested Bristow, "if we find that the front door was unlocked all night, the possibilities broaden."

"How will we find that out?"

"Miss Fulton might remember about it."

"She did mention that," put in Braley; "it was unlocked."

"All the same," insisted Greenleaf, "Morley's got to come back here. Wouldn't you say so?" This question was addressed to Bristow.

The telephone bell rang in the dining room. The chief went to answer it.

"What's that?" Those in the living room heard him. "You? I'm the chief of police. Where are you now? Oh, I see. Come up here, will you? There's been a murder here. Mrs. Withers. Right away? All right; I'll wait for you."

He came back to the living room.

"That was Mr. Henry Morley," he said, "Didn't leave town last night. What do you think of that?"

CHAPTER II

"SOMETHING BIG IN IT"

BEFORE the question was answered the coroner arrived. While Chief Greenleaf told him the circumstances confronting them, Dr. Braley telephoned for a trained nurse for Miss Fulton. In the absence of anybody else to perform the unpleasant task, the doctor went back to take up with the bereaved girl the matter of telegraphing to her family and the details of preparing the murdered woman's body for burial as soon as would be compatible with the plans of the coroner.

"I wonder, Mr. Bristow," suggested Greenleaf, "if I couldn't walk up to your place with you and talk this thing over."

"Glad to have you," agreed Bristow.

The crowd on the porch and in the street began to disperse slowly after the chief had told them none of them could be admitted. In small groups, they made their way to porches or into houses where they lingered, speculating, wondering, advancing impossible theories.

Why had death singled *her* out? Who would ever have suspected that there had been in her life any foothold for tragedy? The secrecy with which she had been struck down, the ease of the murderer's coming and going safely, roused their resentment. They sympathized with themselves as well as with the dead woman.

Confusedly, but at the same time with striking unanimity, they felt that this was not merely a mystery, but a mystery made ugly and shocking by base motives and despicable agents. In common with all mankind, they resented mystery. It emphasized their own dependence on chance. They began to guess at the best method for capturing the guilty.

The chief of police and the lame man had reached the porch of No. 9. There Bristow picked up from a table a scrapbook and a bundle of newspaper clippings. Following him into the living room, Greenleaf brought a paste pot and a pair of shears which the other evidently had been using in placing the clippings in the big book. He put them down on a table in one corner near Bristow's typewriter.

" Still figuring 'em out, I see," he said grimly.

He referred to Bristow's habit of reading murder mysteries in the newspapers and working them out to satisfactory solutions. That was Bristow's way of amusing himself while set down in Furmville for the long struggle to overcome the tuberculosis with which he was afflicted. In fact, as a result of this recreation, he had become known to Greenleaf, who had visited him several times.

He had rendered the captain considerable assistance in a minor case shortly after his arrival in the town, and Greenleaf was really amazed by the correctness of the lame man's solutions of most of the murder cases chronicled. He knew that Bristow had been right on an average of nine times out of ten, often clearing up the affairs on paper many days or even weeks ahead of the authorities in various parts of the country.

Bristow had his records in his scrapbooks to prove his contentions. Under each clipping descriptive of a baffling murder he had written a brief outline of his solving of the case and dated it, following this with the date of the correct or incorrect solutions by the authorities.

"But now," the chief added, as they sat down before the open fire, which earlier had fought against the chill of the cool May morning, "you can work one out right on the ground. And I'll be mighty glad to have your help—if you will help."

"Of course," said Bristow. "I'll be more than glad to make any suggestions I can."

The chief went out on the porch and called across the yard of No. 7 to one of his men on guard at No. 5:

"Simpson, when a young man—name's Morley—gets there and asks for me, tell him to come up here to Number Nine."

He came back and referred to Bristow's offer of help:

"For instance?"

"Well," Bristow answered, "as we see it now, there are three possibilities: Campbell, or Morley, or some unknown man or woman, coloured or white, bent on robbery."

"So far, though, we haven't found any signs of robbery."

"I have."

"What were they?"

"The middle, third and little fingers of Mrs. Withers' left hand were scratched, badly scratched, as if rings had been pulled from them by force. And there was a deep line on the back of her neck. It looked black just now, but it was red when it was inflicted. It was too thin to have been made by a finger, but it might have been caused by somebody's having tugged at a chain about her neck until it broke."

"The thunder you say! I didn't notice any of that."

"I'll show you the marks when we go back there."

"But," objected Greenleaf, "I know Mr. Campbell. He's not the sort to steal. And I don't suppose Morley is."

"They say the same thing about bank presidents," Bristow replied with a slight smile, "but some of them get caught at it, nevertheless."

"Yes; but this is different—unless the murdered woman had extremely valuable jewelry."

"That's true. Besides, if the front door was unlocked all night, or, even if somebody knocked at the door and Mrs. Withers answered it, there is your third possibility, any ordinary robbery and murder."

"I believe that's what will come out," Greenleaf said, his troubled face showing his worried consciousness of inability to handle the situation; "but how will we—how will I prove it?"

"Morley and Campbell can make their own statements."

Bristow, going to the dining room door, called toward the kitchen:

"Mattie!"

Replying to his summons, a middle-aged coloured woman appeared.

"Mattie, didn't I hear Perry tell you yesterday that he was to go to work this morning for Mrs. Withers, 'making' her garden?"

"Yas, suh," answered Mattie, still breathing heavily from her hurried return from No. 5.

"Has he been around this morning?"

"Naw, suh."

"Do you know where Mrs. Withers' servant lives?"

"Yas, suh."

"What's her name?"

"Lucy Thomas, suh."

"Well, I want you to go there right away and find out what's the matter with her, why she didn't show up for work this morning. Take your time. Dinner can wait."

When Mattie had gone, Bristow explained:

"This Perry—Perry Carpenter—is a young negro who does odd jobs in this section. He's about twenty-five, I guess. Each of these bungalows has a garden back of it, you know. There are no houses behind us. I don't like Perry's looks. He did some gardening for me Saturday and yesterday."

"You think he——?"

"He's got a bad face. If neither Campbell nor Morley killed Mrs. Withers, why shouldn't we find out where Perry and the servant woman of Number Five are now, and where they were all last night?"

"I reckon that's right," chimed in Greenleaf. "It looks something like a common darky job at that."

"And this," added Bristow, taking something from his vest pocket and handing it to the chief of police, "looks more like it, doesn't it?"

Greenleaf examined the object the other had put into his hand. It was a metal button of the kind ordinarily worn on overall jumpers, and clinging to it were a few fragments of the dark blue stuff of which overalls are commonly made. On the back of the button were stamped in white the words: "National Overalls Company."

"Where did you get this?" asked the chief.

"I picked it up in the room where the dead girl was; and I'd forgotten it until this minute. It was on the floor a few yards from the body. You saw me when I picked it up. You were at the telephone."

"That's right. I remember now. By cracky! That came off of some darky's working clothes. That's sure!"

"The only trouble is," puzzled Bristow, "your negro doesn't wear overalls at night after he has finished work. He dresses up and loafs down town."

"That's true on Saturday nights. Other nights they don't take the trouble to change. And last night was Monday night. No, sir! That's our first clue, that button; the first sign we've had of the murderer."

"Keep it," Bristow told him. "I'm not as confident as you are, but you might have a look at the blouse of Perry's suit of overalls. We can't overlook anything now."

Deep in thought he gazed at the fire. Greenleaf got up and walked to the window, which gave a magnificent view of the great Carolina mountains in the distance. He was not admiring the mountains, however. He was wondering why Mr. Morley had not arrived.

"By the way," he said, "can't I get a drink of water?"

He was in the dining room on his way to the kitchen before Bristow roused himself from his reverie.

"Wait!" he called to the chief. "Let me get it for you."

Greenleaf, however, had gone into the kitchen. Bristow followed him and took a tumbler from a rack on the wall.

The chief drew the tumbler full twice from the faucet and gulped down the water. His hand shook. He was very nervous.

As they turned to leave the kitchen, he uttered an exclamation and, stooping down swiftly, pulled something from under the stove. When he straightened up, he had in his hand another metal button. He turned it about in his fingers, studying it.

"It looks like the one you found in Number Five," he said.

They compared the two. They were identical. The two men stared at each other.

"What do you make of that?" asked Greenleaf.

"I was wondering," Bristow replied, thinking quickly, "when—how that got there." He paused and added: "Mattie doesn't wear overalls."

They returned to the living room.

"But," he continued, "Perry was working for me yesterday. He was in the kitchen talking to Mattie. I wonder—Well, there's one thing; if Perry's blouse has two buttons missing, he'll be confronted with the job of establishing an alibi for all of last night."

"By cracky!" The captain slapped his hands together in evident relief. "I believe we've got him! I'm going to send a man after him."

He went out to the porch and signalled another of his men.

"Drake," he said, "I want you to find a young negro—name's Perry Carpenter—about twenty-five years old. He does odd jobs around here. Any of these other niggers can tell you where he lives. When you find him, take him to headquarters. Keep him there until I come. Get him. Don't lose him!"

When he stepped back into the house, Bristow was regarding him with a smile.

"I hope you're right," he told the chief, "but I've a hunch you're wrong. I believe this murder is more than an ordinary robbery by a darky. Somehow, I have the impression that there's something big mixed up in it."

"Why?"

"I can't say exactly. Perhaps it's because I've been thinking of the beauty of the victim. Or it may be that I was impressed by what the women said about her when we were waiting for you on the porch."

He thought a while, and decided that he had no explanation of why he had made the remark. He had not meant to say it. It had come from him spontaneously, like an endorsement of what all Manniston Road was saying at that very moment: the "the something big in it" loomed up, intangible but demanding notice.

Greenleaf himself, for all his apparent certainty about the guilt of the negro Perry, sensed vaguely the possibility, the hint, that this crime was even worse than it appeared to be. But he would not admit it. He preferred to keep before his mind the easier answer to the puzzle.

"No," he contradicted Bristow; "I believe Perry's the fellow we want. Here we are dealing with facts, not story-book romances."

Just then a young man sprang up the steps of No. 9 and knocked on the door. It was Henry Morley, come to give weight to Bristow's "hunch."

CHAPTER III

THE RUBY RING

ALTHOUGH it was Chief Greenleaf who opened the door, it was to Bristow that Morley turned, as if he instinctively recognized the superiority of the lame man's personality. Greenleaf, of average height and weight, had nothing of command or domination about him. With his red, weatherbeaten face and mild, expressionless blue eyes, he looked like a well-to-do farmer. He was suggestive of no acquaintance with Tarde, Lombroso or any other authorities on crime and criminals.

"Won't you sit down?" invited Bristow.

The new-comer was tall and slender. In spite of a straight, high-bridged nose and thin lips, his face indicated weakness. His dark-gray eyes had in them either a great deal of worry or undisguised fear. As he took the chair pointed out to him, he was being catalogued by Bristow as showing too much uncertainty, even a womanish timidity. Bristow noticed also that his thick, soft blond hair was carefully parted and brushed, and that his fingers were much manicured.

He breathed in short, quick gasps.

"What is it? How—how did it happen?" he asked, his gaze still on Bristow.

Greenleaf took a seat so that Morley sat between him and Bristow.

"We don't know how it happened," said the chief. "We wanted to know if you could tell us anything."

"I didn't see Mrs. Withers late last night," Morley replied, a nervous tremor in his voice.

"Nobody said you did," commented Bristow.

"No; I know that," Morley agreed in a queer, high voice.

"But you were in the house, Number Five, last evening, weren't you?" Bristow inquired.

"Yes."

"Well, tell us about it."

"I came down here from Washington Saturday," the young man began. "I didn't come to see Mrs. Withers. I came to see Miss Fulton, her sister. Of course, I've seen Mrs. Withers since I've been here; I saw her early last night. You see, last night she went up to the Maplewood Inn for the dinner dance, and, when I called, she was just leaving with a Mr. Campbell. Miss Fulton and I sat on the front porch and in the parlour talking until a little after eleven."

"We understood," put in Bristow, "that Miss Fulton was confined to her bed."

"She was, that is—er—she was supposed to be; but she got up last evening and dressed to receive me."

"I beg your pardon," again interrupted his questioner, "but everything is important here now, and we need information. We have so little of it as yet. I really apologize, but may I ask what your relations with Miss Fulton are?"

Morley hesitated a full minute before he answered.

"If it is to go no further than you gentlemen," he began.

"Of course," the other two agreed.

"Well, then, Miss Fulton and I are engaged to be married."

"Ah! Go ahead." This from the lame man.

"As I said, we talked until a little after eleven. Then I had to leave to catch the midnight train back to Washington."

"But you didn't catch it."

"No. You see, I was stopping at the Maplewood. That's more than a mile from Manniston Road, and it's fully two miles from the railroad station. Somehow, I didn't allow myself enough time, and I missed the train by a bare two minutes."

"What did you do then?"

"What did I do then?"

"Yes—what then?"

"I didn't go back to Maplewood Inn. I took a room for the night at the Brevord Hotel. It's near the station, you know, and I intended to catch the midday train today. Besides, it was late, and I didn't want to take the trouble of walking back or getting a machine to take me back to Maplewood."

He drew out his handkerchief and mopped his forehead, which, as a matter of fact, was perfectly dry. He was tremendously unstrung. Bristow realized this and saw that now, more than at any subsequent time, he would be able to make the young man talk.

"That," he said easily, "accounts for you, doesn't it? Now, I'll tell you. Chief Greenleaf and I are anxious to get some information about the Fulton family. As you know, we people here, being invalids, live pretty much to ourselves. We don't have the strength for much social life, and we don't know much about each other. What can you tell us?"

"Miss Fulton and Mrs. Withers are—were sisters," Morley responded. "Their father, William T. Fulton, is a real estate man in Washington. By the way, Mar—Miss Fulton expects him here this afternoon. She told me so yesterday. Last fall, just before Miss Fulton was taken sick with tuberculosis, he failed, failed for a very large amount of money."

"He was wealthy then?"

"Yes; quite. Mrs. Withers was twenty-five. She married Withers, George S. Withers, of Atlanta, Georgia, when she was twenty-one. But, when Miss Fulton had to come here for her health, Mrs. Withers agreed to come, too, and look after her. Withers isn't wealthy. He's a lawyer in Atlanta, but he hasn't a big income."

"How old is Miss Fulton?" asked Bristow.

"Twenty-three."

"Do you know whether Mrs. Withers had any valuable jewelry—rings, stuff of that kind?"

Morley was for a moment visibly disturbed.

"Why, yes," he answered after a little pause. "When Mr. Fulton failed, Miss Fulton gave up all her jewels, everything, to help meet his debts. Mrs. Withers refused to do this—at least, she didn't do it."

Both Bristow and Greenleaf caught the note of criticism in his voice.

"Just what was the feeling between the two sisters?" pursued Bristow.

Again Morley paused.

"Oh, all right, if you don't feel like discussing that," his interrogator said smoothly. "It's of no consequence. "We'll find out about it elsewhere."

"I suppose I might as well," said Morley. "It really doesn't amount to anything much. There has been considerable coolness between the two women."

"Even when Mrs. Withers was here nursing Miss Fulton?"

"Yes. You see, Mrs. Withers was and always has been Mr. Fulton's favourite. Miss Maria Fulton felt this, and she knew that Mrs. Withers came here only because Mr. Fulton asked her to do it. Also, Miss Fulton never forgave Mrs. Withers for not coming forward with her jewels, jewels which her father had given her—for not coming forward with them when he failed."

"Did they ever quarrel?"

"Well, yes. Sometimes, I think, they did. You know how it is with two women, particularly sisters, who are on what might be called bad terms. Then, as I was about to say, Mrs. Withers wasn't making any sacrifice by being here with her sister. Mr. Fulton, in spite of his reduced means, paid her expenses, all of them. Besides, Mrs. Withers had quite a good time here, going to the dances, and so on."

"Do you know, Mr. Morley, whether they had a quarrel yesterday?"

"They didn't so far as I know."

"Miss Fulton said nothing to you about a quarrel?"

"No."

Bristow was silent a few seconds.

"I think that's all, Mr. Morley. We're much obliged to you. Isn't that all, chief?"

"Yes, for the present," Greenleaf answered with a long breath, thankful the other had been there to do the questioning. "That seems to cover everything."

"I wonder if I could see Miss Fulton," Morley said, rising.

"If the doctor will allow it," Greenleaf told him. "You might go down there and see."

Morley put his hand on the doorknob.

"By the way," interjected Bristow once more, and this time his voice was cold, steely; "Mr. Morley, did you wear rubbers last night?"

"Rubbers?" parroted Morley.

"Yes—rubbers."

Morley stared a moment, as if calculating something.

"Why, yes; I believe I did," he said finally.

Greenleaf, glancing down at Morley's feet, noticed what Bristow had seen three seconds after Morley had entered the room—his feet were large, abnormally large for a man of his build. He must have worn a number ten or, perhaps, a number eleven shoe.

"I thought so," Bristow observed carelessly. "I sleep out on my sleeping porch at the back of the house here, and I knew it rained hard from early in the night until seven this morning."

Morley, without commenting on this, looked at the two men.

"Is there anything more?" he inquired.

"No, nothing more; thanks," said Bristow.

The young man went out quickly, slamming the door in his haste.

Bristow answered Greenleaf's questioning look:

"There was no use in our looking round the outside of the house for possible footprints this morning. If there had been any, the rain would have cleared them away. But, when I first ran up on the porch—it's roofed, like mine here—I noticed the dried marks made by a wet shoe hours before, a large shoe, by a large shoe with a rubber sole, or by a rubber shoe."

"The devil you did!"

"I did.—But it may turn out that Perry, or somebody else, or several other people, wore rubber shoes, or rubber-soled shoes last night. Negroes always have large feet."

"Well, I hope my man's found this Perry nigger," said the chief. "He's the fellow we want."

"And yet," ruminated Bristow, "what young Morley said is interesting enough—two quarreling sisters living together—one decked in jewels, the other deprived of them—the jewels gone this morning." He smiled and waved his hands comprehensively. "As long as it *is* a mystery, let's have it a real mystery. Let's look at all sides of it. There's Perry. There's Morley. And—there's Miss Maria Fulton."

"Miss Fulton!"

"Yes—a possibility."

"Oh, I don't connect her up with it any." The chief's voice was tinged with ridicule.

Bristow answered a knock on the door and opened to admit a uniformed policeman.

"Beg your pardon, chief," said the officer, "but I had something for a Mr. Morley. The men on guard down there at Number Five wouldn't let me in to see him—said I'd better see you."

"What have you got, Avery?" asked Greenleaf.

"It's a little package. You know, I'm on that beat down there. Takes in the Brevord Hotel. The clerk said this Mr. Morley had sent his grips to the station, but had said he was coming up to Number Five, Manniston Road. He said there had been a murder up here. The clerk said he didn't know what to do with this property but turn it over to the police. As soon as I saw what it was, I hurried up here."

"What is it?"

"It's a ring, sir."

"A ring!" exclaimed Bristow. "Let's see it."

Policeman Avery handed Bristow a tissue paper package.

The lame man unwound the paper and discovered a woman's ring, the setting a tremendous pigeon's-blood ruby flanked on each side by a diamond. It was an exceedingly handsome and very valuable piece of jewelry.

"Where did the clerk get this?" Bristow asked swiftly.

For the first time, he was visibly excited.

"A maid found it under the bed on the floor of Mr. Morley's room at the Brevord," answered Avery.

Greenleaf needed no hint from Bristow this time.

"Avery," he said, "your beat takes in the railroad station. Go down to Number Five and get a good look at this man Morley. After that, if he attempts to leave Furmville, arrest him."

CHAPTER IV.

TWO TRAILS

"I'M AFRAID," said Bristow, after the policeman had hurried out, "we made a mistake in permitting Morley to talk to Miss Fulton just at present."

"I can go down there and interrupt them," Greenleaf volunteered.

The lame man reflected, a forefinger against the right side of his nose, the attitude emphasizing the fact that this feature was perceptibly crooked, bent toward the left.

"No," he concluded. "We'd probably be too late." Then he added, "And we didn't find out Morley's employment or profession in Washington—but we can do that later."

The chief of police prepared to leave, saying he was going to call at Douglas Campbell's office and from there go to headquarters in the hope that Perry had been found.

"Can't you come with me?" he invited.

"It's against the doctor's orders," Bristow replied. "He tells me not to leave this house or its porches. If I started to run around with you, I'd be exhausted in an hour. But I'll tell you what: this afternoon, after you've talked to Campbell and the darky, suppose you come back here, and we'll drop down to interview Miss Fulton ourselves."

This surprised Greenleaf.

"You mean you suspect——"

Bristow laughed.

"Oh," he countered lightly, "we've enough suspecting to do already. There's Perry—and there's Morley. Don't let's complicate it too much. But what Miss Fulton has to say may be valuable. By the way, if I should need to do so, how can I persuade anybody that I have authority to ask questions, or to do anything else in this matter?"

The captain thought a moment.

"I'll appoint you to the plain-clothes squad. I appoint you now, and the city commissioners will confirm it. They meet tonight. You're on the force—at a nominal salary—say ten dollars a week. That suit you?"

"Perfectly," consented Bristow. "What I want is the power to help in case I have the opportunity."

Greenleaf went out to the porch, followed by Bristow, and started down the steps.

"By the way," his new employée said in a cautious tone, "don't forget to stop at Number Five and look for those scratches, on the fingers and the neck."

"By cracky!" exclaimed the chief. "I'd forgotten all about it. I'll do that right away."

Looking toward No. 5, Bristow saw a hearse-like wagon drawing up in front of the door. The coroner had already made arrangements for the removal of the body of Mrs. Withers to an undertaking establishment.

The lame man went slowly into the house and stood at the window, staring at the mountains. In the clear, newly washed air, they looked like the soft, tumbling waves of some magically blue sea.

Like most retiring, secluded men, he had his vanity in pronounced degree. He saw himself now, the dominant figure in this city of thirty thousand people, the man who had been selected by the chief of police as the one able to unravel the web of mystery surrounding this startling murder. The thought pleased him, and he smiled. He began to think about himself and about life as a general proposition.

Everything was always so mixed up, so involved. People talked of a divine providence, of the law that virtue is rewarded, of the rule that to do good is to have good done to one. He smiled again. If all that was true, what explanation was there for the murder of this woman, this beauty whose good nature, kindness, and cleverness had endeared her to all with whom she came in contact?

He had heard the women on the porch of No. 5 say that everybody had loved her. Why, then, had some ignorant negro or some white man bent on robbery been permitted to steal up on her in the dead of night and crush out her life? Was there any reason, any logic, any mercy in that?

He drummed on the window-pane with his fingertips and whistled, scarcely audibly, a fragment of tune. His pursed up mouth made it clear that he was not a handsome man—the lower lip was heavy, somewhat protuberant.

Pshaw! There was only one rule of life that held good, so far as he had been able to see. Strength and persistence accomplished things and brought success and security. Weakness and foolish prating about righteousness and virtue were never worth a dollar.

That was it! If you were mighty and clever, you stayed on top. If you were sentimental and looking after other people's interests, you went down. You had no time to bother about the safety and happiness of others. Look out for yourself. Never relent in the fierce battle against the odds of life. That was the only way to conquer and avoid catastrophe.

He was sure of it when he thought about himself. He had a brilliant brain. It was not particularly egotistic for him to think that. It was merely a fact. But he had not used it relentlessly and incessantly. He had relaxed his hold too often when seeking pleasure. Although he had done things which had been applauded by his friends, he had nothing much to show in the way of lasting results.

That was why he was here now, with scarcely enough resources to pay the rent of his bungalow and the expenses of living. A little dabbling in real estate, some third-rate work for the magazines, a passing notoriety as a guesser of crime riddles—it was not a record that promised a bright future.

He sighed. Well, that was the way of life. He might yet accomplish big things although he was under a terrific handicap—and he might not. He would try, and see.

His future was much like the probable outcome of this murder. How would the circumstances shape themselves? What would be the result of circumstantial evidence?

It was all a gamble. Some murderers were lucky and got away. And some innocent men were not lucky. These were like the blundering, illiterate negro Perry. There was an even chance that the guilty man would be caught—and there was an even chance that an innocent man would hang. Life was like that!

He caressed with his forefinger his protruding lip. He wouldn't say the negro was guilty. In spite of the evidence of the buttons, he would advance no such theory yet. And as to Morley—nobody could think that a man with such a weak face would have the nerve to do murder. He knew this. There must be somebody else. It might be that the sister, Maria Fulton, in an excess of rage—But why reason about that before he had talked to her?

It was up to him to fasten the guilt on the guilty man—or woman. That was what was expected of him. And it was a task which——

He turned toward the table and began methodically to paste into their proper places the clippings he had cut from the newspapers concerning other "big" murder cases. He would study them later.

He looked up and saw a very fat man standing just outside the door.

"Hello, Overton," he said, without cordiality, and joined him on the porch.

"I picked out an interesting time to visit you," observed the fat man, still puffing from the exertion of climbing the Manniston Road hill; "what with murder and——"

"And I'm going to be frank with you," Bristow

put in. "I'm helping the police a little, and I haven't the time to gossip now. I know you'll understand——"

"Surely, surely!" said Overton. "I'll come some other time. This sort of stuff's right in your line. You used to be an authority on it in Cincinnati, I remember."

He said good-bye and lumbered awkwardly down the steps. He and Bristow had been good friends in Cincinnati, and he seemed now not at all offended by the summary dismissal.

The door leading from the kitchen to the dining room opened. Mattie had returned. Bristow re-entered the house.

"Well?" he said in the low, kindly tone he used in speaking to her.

"I foun' Lucy Thomas, Mistuh Bristow," she said, breathless and indignant. "She is sho' one sorry nigger. She wuz drunk—layin' out in de parluh uv dat little house uv her'n. Dead drunk."

"Did you wake her up, Mattie?"

"Yas, suh; but she ain' fit to come do no wuk. Dis ole rotten blockade whisky dese niggers drink jes' knocked her out—knocked her out fuh fair."

"Did she say when she got drunk?"

"Las' night, suh, late, wid dat Perry. You know, Mistuh Bristow; he been doin' some wuk fuh you."

"Was Perry drunk last night? Did she tell you?"

"He wuz a little lit up, she says, but he warn't drunk. She didn't have no idea whar he wuz jes' now."

Bristow made no comment on this, and Mattie,

turning slowly away from him, began to mumble something.

"What's that, Mattie?" he asked, only half curious.

"I wuz jes' sayin', Mistuh Bristow, it 'pears to me marveelyus how some uv dese niggers behave. Dey don' look arter de white folks dey wuk fuh. Seems to me marveelyus how a lot uv dem keeps out uv jail."

He was curious enough now.

"What do you mean?" he asked sharply. "What are you talking about?"

"It's jes' dis, suh: when I gits ovuh to Lucy's house, de fus' thing I sees is a key layin' on de flo'. When I ast her 'bout it, she says it mus' be de key to Number Five—she mus' uv drapped it."

"I see," said Bristow thoughtfully. "Yes, you're right, Mattie. There are a lot of careless people in the world."

When she had gone back to the kitchen, the full force of what she had said struck him. How simple it would have been for Perry to have taken the key from the drunken Lucy and gone to No. 5! After the commission of the crime, what would have been easier than for him to throw the key on the floor in Lucy's house, thus apparently proving that he had had no way of gaining entrance to the bungalow?

"I didn't foresee this," he meditated. "There's only one thing more needed to hang that darky. That is the discovery that he has in his possession, or has hidden, the jewelry."

He seemed suddenly reminded of something else by this thought. He went to the telephone and called up the Brevord Hotel.

"A Mr. Morley, Mr. Henry Morley, registered there last night, didn't he?" he inquired of the clerk.

"Yes," the clerk replied.

"I wonder," continued Bristow suavely, "if you'd mind looking at the register and telling me exactly at what time he did register. This is Chief Greenleaf's office talking."

"I see. Yes, sir; very glad to. Just hold the wire a moment while I look."

Bristow waited. The Brevord was scarcely four minutes' walk from the railroad station. Morley, having missed the midnight train by two minutes, should have registered at the hotel certainly not later than ten minutes past midnight.

"I have it," came the clerk's voice. "Mr. Henry Morley, of Washington, D. C., registered here at five minutes past two this morning."

Bristow was astonished, but his voice was uncoloured by surprise when he inquired:

"Are you sure of that?"

"Quite," said the clerk laconically. "We always put down opposite each guest's name the time of arrival and registering."

"Thanks ever so much." Bristow hung up the receiver slowly.

It was now after one o'clock, and, following the routine prescribed by his doctor, he made his way to the sleeping porch to lie down for half an hour before dinner, his midday meal.

"From midnight until two o'clock this morning," he reflected, revolving a dozen different facts in his mind. "Mr. Morley failed to mention how he amused himself during all that time. If he's not a criminal, he's criminally stupid."

CHAPTER V

THE HUSBAND'S STORY

MR. BRISTOW, however, was not allowed to rest half an hour. Instead, he was called upon to consider a phase of the Withers murder more amazing than any of those so far uncovered. Barely ten minutes after his conversation with the clerk of the Brevord, Mattie announced that two gentlemen were waiting to see him, one of them being the chief of police.

When Bristow stepped into the living room, Greenleaf introduced the stranger. He was Mr. Withers—Mr. George S. Withers, husband of the murdered woman. He was of the extreme brunette type, his hair blue-black, his black eyes keen and piercing and always on the move. Bristow got the impression in looking at him that all his features, the aquiline nose, the firm, compressed mouth, the large ears, were remarkably sharp-cut.

The man's excitement was almost beyond his control. He apparently made no attempt to hide the fact that his hands trembled like leaves in the wind and that, every now and then, his legs quivered perceptibly. As soon as he had shaken hands, he sank into a chair.

"Mr. Withers," the chief explained, "caught me at Number Five before I had started down town.

I have explained how you are helping me in this—er—distressing matter. So we came up here."

"I see," said Bristow, betraying no surprise that Withers had appeared so suddenly.

In fact, he had not thought of the husband previously, except to calculate that, in answer to the telegram Dr. Braley had undoubtedly sent, he could not reach Furmville from Atlanta before far into the night.

"He only heard of the tragedy half an hour ago," Greenleaf added.

"I didn't know you were in town or even expected," Bristow said casually. "I thought you were in Atlanta."

"I—I wasn't expected." Withers hurried his words.

"You mean nobody expected you?"

"That's it. I wasn't expected. But I've been in—in town here since yesterday morning."

"And Mrs. Withers didn't know of it?"

"Nobody knew of it. I didn't want anybody to know of it."

Bristow purposely remained silent, awaiting some explanation. He looked down, studying the pattern of the scratches he made by rubbing his right shoe against the side of the built-up sole, two inches thick, of his left shoe. The shortness of his crippled leg made this heavy sole necessary; and the awkwardness of it worried him. He seemed always conscious of it.

Greenleaf, taking his cue from Bristow, said nothing.

"I came in without notifying anybody," Withers

felt himself obliged to continue, "and I registered under an assumed name."

"Where?" the lame man asked swiftly.

"At the Brevord."

"What name—under what name?"

"Waring, Charles B. Waring."

"And you've been in Furmville since yesterday morning? Got here on the eight o'clock train yesterday morning?

"Yes."

Bristow gave him the benefit of another long pause and studied him more closely. He saw that this bereaved husband was of the "high-strung, Southern-gentleman type," hot-tempered, impulsive, one of those apt to believe that "shooting" is the remedy for one's personal ills or injuries. The lines of his mouth betrayed selfishness and peevishness.

The interrogator broke the silence at last:

"Of course, Mr. Withers, there's some good explanation for your secret trip to Furmville?"

"Well—er—yes."

"What is it?"

Withers hesitated.

"I—I don't know that I care to say now—to discuss it yet."

Bristow shot Greenleaf a prompting glance.

"You see, it's this way," the chief acted on the silent suggestion; "I'm in charge of this matter, the capture of the murderer, and Mr. Bristow is helping me. In fact, he's the man in command. His abilities fit him for the work. If the man who killed your wife is caught, it will be through the work of

Mr. Bristow. I'm confident of that. Moreover, every minute we lose now may be disastrous to us. Consequently, we want to hear your story. You appreciate our position, I know."

Withers licked his dry lips with the tip of his dry tongue.

"How about the newspapers?" he asked.

"You'll be talking only for our information," cut in Bristow crisply. "We won't give it to the papers. We want to use it for our own benefit."

"Ah, I see. Well, then——"

Withers got up and paced the length of the floor several times in silence while they watched him. He gave the impression of framing up in advance in his mind what he would say. He seemed to want to talk without talking too much—to tell a part of a story, not all.

"I tell you, gentlemen," he said, going back to his chair, his voice trembling, "this is a hard thing to get to. I mean I don't like to say what I must say. But I see there's no way out but this. The truth of the matter is, I came up here to satisfy myself as to what my wife was doing in regard to a certain matter."

"You mean you were suspicious of her—jealous of her?" Bristow interpolated.

"No, not that," returned the husband.

"He's lying!" was the thought of both Greenleaf and Bristow.

"No. Let me make that very clear. I never doubted her in that way."

"Well, how did you doubt her?"

Withers winced.

"I don't mean I doubted her at all. I mean I thought she was being imposed upon financially. In fact, I was sure of it. I'm sure of it now."

"You mean blackmail?" Bristow narrowed down the inquiry.

"Just that. And I'll tell you about it." He rasped his dry lips again. "This sort of thing, this blackmail, had happened to her twice before this. Once it was when she was at Atlantic City for a month with her sister, Miss Maria Fulton.

"That was a year after our marriage. Then, two years later—just about a year ago now—when she was in Washington visiting her father and sister. Both those times things happened as they had begun to happen here, in fact as they've been happening here for the past two months."

"Well," Bristow urged him on, "what happened?"

"She got away with too much money, more money than she could possibly have used for herself in any legitimate way. First, she got her father to give her all she could get out of him. Her second step would be to write to me for all I could spare, making flimsy excuses for her need of it.

"Her third resource was to pawn all her jewels. She pawned them on these first two occasions I've described. I say she pawned them, but I never had definite proof of it. However, I was sure of it. I don't know that she had come to this in Furmville. If she hadn't she would have."

"What were Mrs. Withers' jewels worth?"

"Originally, I should say, they cost about fifteen thousand dollars. She had no difficulty, I suppose, in raising six or seven thousand dollars on them—even more than that."

"They were worth so much as all that?"

"Yes. Her father had given her most of them before his business failure. He failed last fall, I forgot to mention."

"Now," Bristow said persuasively, "about this blackmailing proposition. What was—what is your idea about that?"

Withers produced and lit a cigarette, handling it with quivering fingers.

"Somebody, some man, had a hold of some sort on her. Whenever he needed money, had to have money, he got it from her. That is, he did this whenever he could find her away from home. So far as I know, he never tried to operate in Atlanta."

"What do you think this hold was?"

"Well," Withers began, and paused.

"Your theories are perfectly safe with us," Bristow reassured him.

"I thought, naturally, that it had something to do with her life previous to the time I met her."

"How?"

"I didn't know. That's what worried me." All of a sudden, his hearers got a clear idea of what the man had suffered. It was plainly to be detected in his voice. "It might have been a harmless love affair, a flirtation, with letters involved, letters which she thought would distress me if I ever saw them."

"Nothing more than that?"

"I never thought she had been guilty of anything—well, immoral, heinous."

"You say," Bristow changed the course of questioning, "she pawned her jewels twice. How did she do that? Where did she get the money to redeem them after the first pawning?"

"I don't know. I never could find out."

"You had no six or seven thousand dollars to give her for that purpose, as I understand it?"

"No."

"Where did she get it, then?" Bristow's questions, despite their directness, were free from offense.

"I—I thought," Withers began again and paused. "I thought that, perhaps, her father helped her out, got the jewels out of pawn both times for her."

"Did you ever ask him?"

"Yes; and he denied having done so. But, you see, my theory is borne out. Before, when she pawned them, her father was wealthy; and she was his favourite child. She knew he would help her. But now his money is gone. He's failed. Consequently, she has not pawned them this time. She knew there would be no chance to redeem them."

Bristow leaned forward in his chair.

"Mr. Withers," he asked, "as a matter of fact, did you ever know that your wife had pawned her jewels?"

"Well," he said, as if making an admission, "she would never confess it to me. I assumed it from the fact that on both occasions the jewels were missing for a good while. They were certainly not in her possession. She couldn't produce them when called upon to do so."

"I see. Now, Mr. Withers, what did you do yesterday, all day yesterday, after reaching here?"

"I went to the Brevord and registered under the name of Waring. After I had had breakfast, I went straight to Abrahamson's pawnshop. It's the only pawnshop in town. I told him I was looking for some stolen jewelry and I expected that an attempt might be made to pawn it with him. He agreed to let me wait there, well concealed by the heavy hangings at the back of his shop. I spent the day there except for a few minutes in the afternoon when I went out for a quick lunch."

"Yes? Did you find out anything?"

Once more Withers found it hard to speak.

"Yes"; he said finally. "A man came in and pawned one of my wife's rings. It had a setting of three diamonds. It was worth about seven hundred and fifty dollars, I should say. Abrahamson let him have only a hundred on it."

"Why only a hundred?"

"I had asked him to do that, so as to prove that the man was a thief—you know, willing to take anything offered to him."

"And he did take the hundred?"

"He did."

"What happened after that?"

"I followed him from the shop—for half a block. When he had gone that distance, I lost him. He stepped into a store, and I waited for him to come out. He never did. It was the old dodge. The store extended the width of a block. He made his escape through the other entrance."

Greenleaf was more excited even than Withers.

"This man," the chief put in; "what did he look like?"

"He was of average weight, medium height. He had a gold tooth, the upper left bicuspid gold. His nose was aquiline. He wore a long, dark gray raincoat, and he had a cap with its long visor pulled well over his face. Then, too, he wore a beard, chestnut-brown in colour. That's about the best description I can give you of him. You see, this happened late in the afternoon."

"All right," Bristow kept to the main thread of the story. "Now, about last night. What then?"

Withers threw away his cigarette and sighed.

"I came up here and watched Number Five. I had an idea that this fellow might show up."

"Did he?"

"No."

"Where did you watch from?"

"Most of the time I sat on the steps of Number Four, almost directly across the road from Number Five. You know how it is on this street. Nearly everybody is in the back of the house after dark. The invalids are on the sleeping porches behind the houses. Besides, it was in deep shadow where I was. I was not observed when my—when Mrs. Withers left the house with an escort, a man, early in the evening."

"And you waited until she returned?"

"Yes; I waited."

"Very well." There was for the first time a hint of sharpness in Bristow's voice. "You waited. What did you see?"

For the past few minutes a change had been taking place in the bearing of Withers. It was as if, having recovered slightly from the terrific shock of his wife's death, he was gradually stiffening, gaining the strength necessary to withstand the swift volley of Bristow's questions.

The questioner, sensing this alteration in the other, made his queries all the quicker and more peremptory. He wanted to profit as much as possible from the other's lack of control.

"I saw her return with her escort," Withers answered. "She shook hands with him and went into the house and closed the door. He got into his machine, turned it and went back toward town."

"Was his machine noisy?"

"No."

"Did you try to enter Number Five?"

"No. I wasn't ready to disclose my presence. I wanted more time."

He put his hand to his watch pocket and was surprised to find that no watch was there; he had been making nervous little movements like that throughout the interview; but he kept his keen glance on his questioner.

"Then, tell us this, please," Bristow demanded, the sharpness in his tone pronounced: "have you and your wife been on the best of terms lately? And another thing: have you ever had any lasting, distressing disagreements with her?"

The effect of this upon Withers was entirely surprising. He sprang from his chair, his features suddenly working with rage.

"Dammit!" he exclaimed in a tense, vibrant voice, as his glance rested first on Bristow and then on Greenleaf. "What does all this amount to anyway? Here you are, asking me questions as if you thought I had killed my own wife! What I want is results, not a lot of hot air and bluff!"

He snapped his fingers under Bristow's nose.

"Why, dammit!" he shrilled. "Haven't you any idea yet where to look for the murderer? Are you groping around here helplessly after all this time? Dammit! I want a real detective on this job, and I'm going to get one."

He clapped his felt hat to his head and started toward the door.

"You can bet your last dollar on that! I'm going to get one, and he'll be here tomorrow if telegrams can bring him. I'll have Sam Braceway, the cleverest fellow in this business in the South, here tomorrow! I intend to have punishment for the devil who killed my wife. Punishment!—the worst kind!"

His lips were trembling, and he dashed the back of his hand across his face, as if he feared the formation of tears in his eyes.

"You two boneheads can put that in your pipes and smoke it! I mean business!"

He slammed the door, and was gone, taking the steps to the street in two bounds.

"By cracky!" said Greenleaf. "What do you make of that?"

"Nothing," Bristow answered contemptuously; "nothing except that it may be well for us to find out a whole lot more about Mr. Withers and his peculiarities of temper and temperament."

"I should say so," the chief chimed agreement.

"Of course," Bristow added, "that was the easiest way for him to break off our inquiry. I don't think he was on the level with all that storming and raging. It might have been just a great big bluff—that's all. And yet, that Braceway he talked about is good, a wonder. He's done some wonderful work."

"Here's one point," Greenleaf advanced: "why didn't he ask for help from the police yesterday afternoon when he lost track of that fellow with the gold tooth?"

"Yes," the other returned absent-mindedly; "why didn't he?"

CHAPTER VI

MORLEY IS IN A HURRY

BRISTOW looked at his watch. It was nearly half-past two o'clock.

"Hear anything about Perry?" he asked.

"Yes," Greenleaf informed him. "My man found him. They've got him down at headquarters. I phoned from Number Five and got this. He'd been drinking. I gather that he's about half-drunk now."

"Good! If he'll talk at all, it will be easier for you to get the truth out of him that way than if he were cold sober. Suppose you see him and Douglas Campbell; and later on this afternoon you and I can talk to Miss Fulton and her father."

"Her father won't be here today. He wired that a little while ago. He'll get here early in the morning."

"Very well. It's of no consequence just now. Come back here for me at four, will you?"

When the chief had gone, Bristow sat down to his delayed dinner. As he ate, he went over the facts so far discovered, and catalogued them:

Perry, the negro—incriminated, probably, by the buttons from his overalls jacket; by the ease with which he could have obtained from Lucy Thomas the kitchen key to No. 5; by the possible motive of robbery; and by the brutal means, choking, employed to inflict death.

Morley—incriminated by his unknown whereabouts during the two hours following his missing the midnight train, and by the discovery of the ring (possibly Mrs. Withers') in his room at the Brevord.

Withers—involved by the probable motive of jealousy and rage, and by his secret trip to Furmville.

Maria Fulton—well, he would see.

"Just now," he concluded in his own mind, "it looks worse for the negro than anybody else. There's one thing certain: the man against whom the most evidence rests by the time they have the inquest tomorrow will be the one held for the action of the grand jury. That's the thing to do—get the one who seems most probably guilty."

He thought of Douglas Campbell and immediately dismissed him as a possibility in the list of probable murderers. The young real estate dealer had been completely exonerated by the statement of the dead woman's husband: that, upon bringing her back to the bungalow, he had at once said good night to her and gone home.

Nor did he puzzle his mind about the unknown individual with the gold tooth, he who had appeared in Abrahamson's pawnshop and a few minutes later miraculously disappeared. If the ring pawned had belonged to Mrs. Withers, why should this man return to No. 5 and murder her? If he had obtained nothing from her beforehand, he might have had a real motive for the crime. But, since he had already got the ring, it seemed folly to assume that he would later kill her.

In spite of his growing belief that the onus of proof must fall upon the negro, Bristow could not keep his thoughts away from young Morley. He, more than any of the other suspects, had told an unsatisfactory story. Besides, he had a bad face.

The latest addition to the Furmville plain-clothes squad remembered how carefully Morley's hands had been manicured. He——

With a quick motion, he went to the telephone and called for Greenleaf.

"Chief, are you still holding Perry?"

"Sure, I'm holding him. I'll continue to hold him for some time, I'm thinking. His story don't suit me. He says——"

"All right. I'll get that from you when I see you this afternoon. In the meantime, I wish you'd have his finger nails carefully cleaned. I want——"

But the request had instantly overwhelmed Greenleaf.

"What!" he yelled. "Clean his finger nails!"

"Yes," Bristow continued smoothly, disregarding the other's evident distaste and surprise. "If I were down there, I'd do it myself. In fact, it would be better for you to do it. Don't leave it to some careless subordinate."

The chief laughed his sarcasm.

"You know," this still with laughter, "we Southerners are none too strong on acting as manicures to these coloured folks."

"It's absolutely necessary," was the insistent answer. "And, when you do clean them, save every bit of dirt thus obtained. Now, will you do it?"

"Why, yes," Greenleaf assented with reluctance. "If you say it's absolutely necessary, I'll do it—I'll do it myself."

"Good. I'll depend on you for it. By the way, can't you have somebody, your man Jenkins or some one as good as he is, go out on a real hunt for the fellow with the gold tooth? You remember Withers' description of him?"

"Yes. I'd thought of that."

"That's good. If he can't spot him at any of the hotels, have him make the rounds of the boarding houses. I think you'd like to get your hands on a customer as slippery as Withers says that man is."

"I'll send Jenkins at once," the chief took his directions in good part.

"Good again. By the way, you'll be up here at four?"

"No; five. Dr. Braley told me we'd have to wait until then; said we'd better. He wants her to get that extra hour's sleep."

Bristow started to say something further, hesitated and then hung up the receiver with a word of assent.

Mattie had come in to clear off the table.

"Go down to Number Six," he told her, "and ask Mrs. Allen if she will be so kind as to come up here at her earliest convenience. Explain to her that it's against the doctor's orders for me to leave this house, and that the excitement of this morning has tired me out."

Mrs. Allen appeared in less than a quarter of an hour. He received her in the living room and introduced himself, apologizing for not having been able to call on her. She understood perfectly, she said.

She was a woman about forty years of age, her face a little thin and worn, a good deal of gray in her dark hair. She had been nursing her husband for two years, and the strain had begun to tell. Nevertheless, he soon saw that she was a woman of refinement, possessed of a keen intelligence.

"I wish," he requested, after he had explained his connection with the murder, "you'd tell me all you know about these sisters. I gathered this morning that you were well acquainted with them."

He had always found it easy to gain the confidence of women. They liked his manners, his air of deference, his manifest interest in everything they said.

"I can't say that I've been intimate with them," Mrs. Allen explained in her soft, pleasing voice; "but Mrs. Withers and I knew each other pretty well. She came over to my house quite frequently, and I was in the habit of running in to see her."

"Don't you know the other, Miss Fulton, equally well?"

"No. You see, she was always in, or on, the bed, and she never seemed to want to talk. Besides, she was different from Mrs. Withers—not so bright and attractive, and not so neighbourly."

"Mrs. Withers was always a laughing, sparkling sort of a person, wasn't she?"

"She gave that impression to some people," Mrs. Allen answered thoughtfully, "but not to me. It was her nature to be free and happy. Most of the time she seemed that way. But there were other times when I could see that she had something weighing on her mind, something depressing her."

"Ah!" Bristow said with deeper interest. "That's just what we want to find out about."

Mrs. Allen sat silent for a moment pursing her lips. Bristow let her reflect.

"I don't think," she said at last, "Mrs. Withers ever was in fear of anybody or any thing. She wasn't that kind."

"Did she ever tell you anything to make you think that she wasn't happy?"

"I was trying to recall just what it was. Once, I remember, when she was sitting out on the sleeping porch—she sometimes came out there to talk to my husband, who is always in bed—we had been discussing the care with which every woman had to live her life.

"'Women are like politicians,' Mr. Allen said. 'They can't afford to have a dark spot in their past. If they do, somebody will drag it out.'

"At that Mrs. Withers cried out:

"'Oh! how awfully true that is! And how unfair! It never seems to matter with men, but with women it means heaven, or the other thing. I wish I knew——' She broke off with a gasp, and I saw her lip tremble.

"It was funny, but at the time I thought she was referring to her sister, not to herself."

"What made you think that?"

"I don't know. I had no real reason for it. Perhaps it was just because unhappiness seemed so foreign to Mrs. Withers herself."

"Was there anything else?"

"Once, when I ran into Number Five, I found her crying. She was in the living room, all doubled up in a rocking chair, crying silently."

"Did she say why?"

"No; but, while I was trying to soothe her, she said, 'Life's so hard—it's so hard to straighten out a tangle when once you've made it. If one could just go back and do things over again!' When I asked her if I could help her, she said I couldn't. 'Nobody can,' she sobbed out on my shoulder. 'It doesn't concern me alone. I'll have to fight it out the best way I can.'"

Bristow was greatly interested.

"What did you conclude from all that, Mrs. Allen?" he asked.

"My impression was very vague," Mrs. Allen returned frankly. "I don't think it is of much value now. I got, somehow, the idea that there was in her life something which she had to conceal, something which might at any moment be discovered. I thought she was worrying about its effect on her husband. Of course, though, that was just my idea."

"I see. Now, just one other thing: what did you think, what do you think, of Miss Fulton?"

"Oh, merely that she's bad-tempered and impatient, always complaining. She was totally without any appreciation of all that Mrs. Withers did for her. Nobody likes Miss Fulton particularly. I think all of us, as we came to know the two, were amazed that Mrs. Withers could have such a disagreeable sister."

Mrs. Allen's recital, while interesting and valuable as to Mrs. Withers' acknowledgment that she felt compelled to keep secret some part of her life, threw no practical light on the situation.

Bristow was silent, thoughtful, for a few moments.

"I've never seen Miss Fulton, except for the glance I had at her this morning," he said. "Was it possible for anybody to mistake one for the other? I mean this: if a man had known that last night Miss Fulton was up and dressed, could it have been possible for him, in a dim light and under the stress of terrific agitation, to have attacked Mrs. Withers under the impression that he was attacking Miss Fulton?"

"Oh, no!" Mrs. Allen said emphatically, and then added: "Oh, I see what you mean. Well, they were of about the same build, although Mrs. Withers wasn't so thin as Miss Fulton is. Then, their hair is different, Mrs. Withers' black, Miss Fulton's blond. I don't know. I should say it all depended on how dark it was."

When Mrs. Allen had gone, Bristow took from a bookcase one of his scrapbooks and went to work pasting into place the clippings he had been reading that morning when interrupted by the cry of murder.

For nine years he had been studying murder cases and the methods of murderers. People had laughed at his fad, but now he was more pleased with himself as a result of it than ever before. He was still pleasantly aware of the prominence he would enjoy in Furmville because of Greenleaf's having called on him for assistance.

"Every murderer," he had said many times, "makes some mistake, big or little, which will lead to his destruction if the authorities have brains enough to find it."

He thought the rule might apply too widely to this case. In fact, his own trouble now was that too many mistakes had been made, too many clues had been left lying around. In order to determine the guilty person, much chaff would have to be sifted from the wheat of truth.

He was closing his scrapbook when the chief of police arrived a few minutes before five o'clock.

"Henry Morley," Greenleaf announced at once, "is a receiving teller in a bank in Washington—the Anderson National Bank."

"And receiving tellers," put in Bristow quickly, "sometimes need money—need it to make good other money they have 'borrowed' from the bank. How did you find this out?"

"He told me when I met him at Number Five after leaving you this afternoon."

"Was he still there then?"

"Yes. It seems that Miss Fulton refused at first to see him. When she did see him, it was for only a minute or two. He was very much agitated when he came from her room."

"There's another thing," added Bristow. "Morley has two hours of last night to account for. He told us he missed the midnight train and went to the Brevord to spend the night. As a matter of fact, he registered at the Brevord a little after two o'clock this morning."

The chief's jaw dropped.

"How do you know that?"

"I called up the Brevord and got the information from the clerk."

"That settles it, then," Greenleaf said, his jaw set. "That young man will have to remain with us for a while."

"Yes; quite properly."

"I guess it's time for us to move." The chief turned toward the door.

"One moment," said the other. "Somehow, I have the impression that we may get important stuff from Maria Fulton. She may not give it to us directly and willingly, but we may get it all the same. And I was thinking this: you and I have got to keep our heads. We don't want to get rattled with the idea that we're up against an unsolvable mystery.

"As you know, I've lived in New York and Chicago and Cincinnati. For the past eight or nine years I've gotten a lot of fun out of watching and studying these cases. And the thing I've learned above all others is that the best way for a criminal to escape is for the authorities to lose their heads and think they are up against something that's really much bigger than it is.

"You see what I mean? What we want to do

is to go ahead with our eyes open, knowing that at any moment we may stumble against the one act that will make everything clear and definite."

"That's good talk, and I'll try to act on it," replied the chief, "but, gee whiz! I'm not used to stuff of this sort. It kinder makes me sick."

They went out to the porch.

"By the way," Bristow asked, "what about the two buttons we found?"

"They belonged to Perry," Greenleaf answered. "There's no getting around that. He had the two middle buttons of his overalls jacket missing. What's more, one of the buttons, the one that had a little piece of the cloth clinging to it, fitted exactly into the hole made in the jacket when the button was pulled out."

"Which button was that?"

"The first one—the one you found in Number Five."

They started down the steps.

"You saw the scratches on Mrs. Withers' hand, didn't you?" said Bristow.

"Yes."

"Well, if Perry did the scratching, we can prove it. Any good laboratory man can tell us whether the stuff that was under his nails contains particles of the human skin, the epidermis. If those particles are found, the case is settled, it seems to me."

"By cracky!" exclaimed Greenleaf, his admiration of his assistant growing. "You've solved the problem—gone to the very bottom of it."

"What did Perry have to say? What was his story?"

"Oh, it amounted to nothing. Said he wasn't near Number Five; said he was drunk last night and thought he was at the house of this Lucy Thomas all the time."

"Then, the proof rests upon what the laboratory analysis of the finger nail stuff shows. When can we get that report?"

Bristow was a little surprised by the embarrassment Greenleaf showed before answering:

"We can get it tomorrow—by wire."

"Why can't we get it tonight—or tomorrow at the latest? The Davis laboratory here can do the work. It does laboratory work for all these doctors here."

"It can't do any work for me," objected Greenleaf stubbornly. "Dr. Davis and I aren't on speaking terms, personally or politically. I'll send the stuff down to a laboratory at Charlotte. It will reach there tomorrow morning if I get it off on the midnight train. We can get the telegraphed report on it late tomorrow or the day after."

"All right; I guess that will do," agreed Bristow.

As they started up the steps to the Fulton bungalow, Morley came out to the porch and charged down toward them. His face was convulsed as if by anger or fear. He did not seem to see the two men. Bristow caught him by the arm and put the query:

"Where are you going, Mr. Morley?"

Morley shook off his hand and answered curtly:

"To Washington. I've barely got time to catch my train."

"Don't hurry," Bristow said with a touch of sarcasm. "You're too good at missing trains anyway. Besides, we want to know what you did between midnight and two-ten this morning, and why you failed to tell us this morning that you didn't register at the Brevord until after two."

Morley's face went white.

"There wasn't anything to that," he explained. "I didn't mean to conceal anything. I didn't go anywhere—anywhere specially."

"Where did you go?" insisted Bristow.

"I took a walk. That was all. I didn't feel like sleeping."

"Did you see anybody while you were walking?"

"Not that I remember. Why?"

"Because, if you did, it might be advisable for you to remember. It may become necessary for you to prove an alibi."

"Oh, that!" the young man said with a nervous laugh.

"Yes. Can't you tell us where you went?"

"I wandered around, up and down the downtown streets. That was all."

"Well, remember," Bristow cautioned him. "If you can produce two or three people who saw you down there, it may help you a whole lot."

"Oh, that's all right. I haven't done anything against the law. The idea's absurd."

"Mr. Bristow's right," Greenleaf put in. "We'll have to know more about how you spent those two hours. Really, we will. If you try to leave town, you'll be arrested. My men have their orders."

Greenleaf had forgotten about the ring found in the young man's hotel room, but Bristow hadn't.

Morley went slowly down Manniston Road. There was a cold moisture upon his forehead.

CHAPTER VII

MISS FULTON IS HYSTERICAL

THE chief and his assistant were received by Miss Kelly, the trained nurse. Bristow wasted no time in what he considered to be the crucial search for more evidence. In speaking to her he exercised all his persuasiveness, all the suggestion of power and authority that he could force into his voice and expression. And yet, he gave her, as he had given Mrs. Allen, the impression that he deferred to her and prized her opinions.

"Isn't there something you can tell us?" he asked, holding her glance with his own.

"What do you mean?"

She was a strong, capable-looking woman of twenty-six years or so.

"Like every good citizen," he answered smoothly, "you want exactly what we want, a clearing up of all this muddle. I thought, perhaps, there might be something you'd heard or seen. Isn't there?"

"No; nothing, sir," she returned, true to her professional teaching that a nurse is forbidden to reveal the secrets of the sickroom.

"You'll be called as a witness at the inquest," he hazarded, and was rewarded by a look of uncertainty in her eyes. "Your duty to the law is above everything else," he added.

"I've heard Miss Fulton say only one thing," she admitted reluctantly. "She's said it several times while under the influence of the sedatives she's had."

"What was it?"

"Nothing that made any sense. It was, 'When he—say—I—asleep.' There were long pauses between each of the words. She said it four or five times. But she hasn't said anything since she waked up."

"How long has she been awake?"

"About fifteen minutes. Mr. Morley saw her five minutes ago, but he wasn't in there more than a minute or two."

"Morley's seen her a second time!"

"Yes; but each time she hasn't wanted to talk to him. The truth is, she drove him out of the room."

"You didn't hear what they said?"

Miss Kelly drew herself up indignantly.

"I wasn't in the room," she said coldly. "Of course, I didn't hear."

Bristow apologized for the implication that she had overheard intentionally.

When he and Greenleaf were shown into Miss Fulton's room, he had made up his mind in lightning-like manner that what she had said in her delirium meant: "When he (her father or the police) asks me about last night, I shall say I was asleep all night." It came to him like an intuition, without his even trying to reason it out; and he decided to act on it.

They found Maria Fulton propped up against

pillows in the bed. Although her pupils were still enlarged by the sedatives she had had, she was plainly labouring under the stress of great emotion.

Bristow was pleased by that. It would make it easier to learn what she knew. It is difficult, he reflected, for a person under the partial effects of a drug to lie intelligently or convincingly.

He and Greenleaf, taking the chairs that had been placed near the bed by Miss Kelly, regretted the necessity of their intrusion.

"Oh, it's all right," Miss Fulton said petulantly. "I know it's essential. Dr. Braley told me so."

Bristow studied her intently. He saw that Mrs. Allen had been right. Maria Fulton was a dissatisfied, peevish woman. She had the heavy, slightly pendent lower lip that goes with much pouting. There was the constant trace of a frown between her eyebrows, and in the eyes themselves was the look of complaint and protest which the "martyr-type" woman always shows.

She was of the infantile, spoiled class, he decided, one who, remembering that her childhood tears and fits of temper had always resulted in her getting what she wanted, had brought the habit into her adult years. He noted, too, that her gorgeous ash-blond hair had been carefully "done," piled in high masses above her petulant face.

"There are just a few questions which we thought it imperative to ask you," he said, trying to convey to her his desire to be as considerate as possible. "We shall make them as brief as we can."

Miss Fulton plucked impatiently at the coverlet, but said nothing.

Bristow, acting on his belief that life with this girl must always be more or less stormy, took a chance.

"Now," he said, fixing his keen glance upon her, "about this quarrel you and your sister had yesterday?"

She frowned and waved her right hand in careless dismissal of the subject.

"Oh, that," she said, "didn't amount to anything."

"What was it about?"

"I really don't know. You see, my sister and I didn't get along very well together."

Bristow put out his hand, and Greenleaf handed him the ring that had been found in Morley's room at the Brevord.

"This ring," he said; "whose is it?"

She sat up straight and gasped. Her pallor grew. Even her lips went thoroughly white.

"Where did you get that?" she asked huskily.

"It doesn't matter. Whose is it?"

"It—it was my sister's," she said, almost in a whisper.

"Do you know who gave it to Mr. Morley?"

She stared, speechless, at Bristow.

"Don't you know?" he persisted.

"Yes," she said with obvious effort; "I—I lent it to him."

"When?"

"Yest—last night."

"Why?"

She tried to smile, but her features were moulded more nearly to a grimace.

"Mr. Morley and I—and I—have been engaged," she laboured to explain. "He said he wanted to wear it for a while just because it belonged to me."

"But he knew it didn't belong to you, didn't he?"

"I suppose," she corrected herself, "he meant he wanted to wear it because I had worn it."

"I see," commented Bristow, and added very quickly: "How much of your sister's jewelry is in this house now?"

Miss Fulton stared at him again, and did not answer.

"Can't you tell me?" he urged. "How much?"

She turned her head from him and looked out of the window.

"None of it," she replied finally. "I had Miss Kelly look for it. It's all—gone."

"Why did you have Miss Kelly look for it? What made you suspect that it was gone?"

She turned to him and frowned more deeply, angrily.

"It was, I suppose," she said shortly, "the first and most natural suspicion for any one to have; that, since she had been killed, she had been robbed. It was the only motive of which I could think."

"Yes," he agreed pleasantly, handing the ring back to the chief; "I think you're right there."

He was silent for a full minute while the girl in the bed plucked at the coverlet and eyed first him and then Greenleaf.

"Miss Fulton," he demanded more sharply than

he had yet spoken, "did you see or hear anything last night in connection with this tragedy, the death of your sister?"

"No; nothing," she answered, her voice now approaching firmness. It was a firmness, however, that was forced.

"How do you explain that?"

"I went to bed before my sister returned from the dinner dance, and I had taken something Dr. Braley had given me that breaks up the severe coughing attacks to which I am subject and that also puts me to sleep."

"Makes you sleep soundly?"

"Very."

"It was a hypodermic injection, wasn't it?"

"Yes."

"And you took it—administered it to yourself?"

"Yes."

"Do you know what it was?"

"Yes; morphine."

"A sixteenth of a grain, wasn't it? That's what is always given to tuberculars to prevent violent spells of coughing, isn't it?"

She hesitated, but finally assented.

"But that's very little to make one sleep so soundly, that one couldn't hear the cries of a woman being murdered and all the noises that must have accompanied the attack upon her. Don't you think so?"

"But, you must remember," she said tartly, "I'm not accustomed to taking morphine. Anyway, that's the way it affected me."

"You heard absolutely nothing and saw nothing

until you discovered your sister's body at ten o'clock this morning?"

"That's true. Yes; that's true." She looked out of the window, paying him no more attention.

Bristow, in his turn, was silent. Greenleaf took up the inquiry:

"Several times today, while you were asleep or delirious, you said the words: 'When he—say—I—asleep.' Can you explain that for us, Miss Fulton?"

Her pallor deepened. This time terror flourished in her eyes as she turned sharply toward Greenleaf.

"Who says I said that?" she demanded, husky again.

"Things are heard pretty easily in these bungalows," he said. "One of my men heard it."

"Oh, I understand," she replied, a hint of craftiness creeping into her voice. "No; I can't explain it. One can't often explain one's ravings."

"It merely suggested something that we had thought impossible," Bristow interjected soothingly: "that you might have wanted to deny having heard something which you really did hear; that you were protecting somebody."

"Oh," she said angrily, "that's absurd—utterly."

"Quite," lied Bristow suavely. "That was what I told Chief Greenleaf. "Then, with sharp directness, he asked her: "Who do you think killed your sister?"

"I don't know! Oh, I don't know!" she cried shrilly, more than ever suggestive of the spoiled child.

"It must have been some burglar. She was very popular, everybody said. She had no enemies."

"None at all?"

"None that I know of."

"But Mr. Morley didn't like her, did he?"

"No," she said slowly. "He didn't like her, but you couldn't have called him her enemy."

Bristow moved his chair toward her several inches.

"Miss Fulton," he asked, "you and Mr. Morley are engaged to be married, aren't you?"

"No!" she surprised him. "No; we're not!"

He did not tell her that Morley had said they were.

Greenleaf was now clearly conscious of what he had vaguely felt while listening to Bristow's questioning of Withers: the lame man had the faculty of seeming entirely inoffensive in his queries but at the same time putting into his voice an irritating, challenging quality which was bound to work on the feelings of the person to whom he talked. He had begun to have this effect on Miss Fulton.

"I understood," he informed her, "that you were —er—quite fond of each other."

"Not at all! Not at all!" she denied with increasing vehemence. "I'm not engaged to him now. Nothing could induce me to marry him!"

"Mr. Morley declared this morning that you and he were to be married."

She caught herself up quickly, anger evident in her eyes, and at the same time, also, a look of caution. Bristow decided she wanted to tell nothing, to give him no advantage, no actual insight into the clouded situation.

"I see what you mean," she said. "We were engaged, but I finally decided that our marriage was impossible—because of this—my illness."

"And you told him so?"

She thought a long moment before she answered: "Yes."

"When?"

"Yesterday."

"Then, when did you give him—let him have Mrs. Withers' ring?"

She showed signs of weakening.

"Yesterday," she declared. "No! Last night, I've already told you."

"And why did he want the ring last night when you had broken with him earlier yesterday?"

His subtle irritation of her by his manner and tone had unstrung her at last.

"I don't know," she cried, hysterics in her voice. "Oh, I don't know! Why do you ask me all these foolish little questions?" She tore unconsciously at the counterpane, her fingers writhing against one another. "Please, please don't bother me any more! Leave me! Leave me now, won't you?"

The high, shrill quality of her tone brought Miss Kelly into the room.

"I think," the nurse said, "you gentlemen will have to put off further conversation with Miss Fulton—if you can. The doctor said she was not to be subjected to too much excitement."

They already had risen.

"We've very much obliged to you, Miss Fulton,"

Bristow said in his pseudo-pleasant way. "It may be useful to us to know about you and Mr. Mor——"

He was interrupted by a cry from the girl. Without the slightest warning, she had lost the last shred of her self-control. She began to beat on the covering of her bed with clenched fists. He could see how her whole body moved and twisted.

Greenleaf, startled by the girl's demeanour, moved further from her. Bristow stood his ground, watching her closely.

She glared at him with the wild look that frequently comes to the hysterical or neurotic woman's eyes. She did not seem to be suffering. She was angry, carried away by her rage, and giving vent to it without any attempt at restraint!

In two or three seconds she had become suggestive of an animal, her nostrils distended, the upper lip drawn back from her teeth. Bristow, going beyond surface indications, estimated her at her true worth: "Too much indulged; overshadowed, perhaps, by some older member of the family; but capable of big things, even charm. She's far from being a nonentity. She may help me yet."

He regarded her calmly, and smiled.

"Don't mention him to me again!" she screamed. "I won't have it! I won't have it, I tell you! I never want to see him again—never! Don't speak the name of Henry Morley in——"

But Miss Kelly had quickly motioned them out and closed the door. Even on the outside, however, they could hear her shrill, whining protest against any mention of Morley.

"Now!" said Greenleaf as they went through the living room. "What do you make of that?"

They left the house and stood on the sidewalk outside.

"Not much," Bristow replied, thinking deeply. "What with Withers throwing a fit, and then this girl having, or shamming, hysterics, it's disappointing. But here's a question: what has Morley done since last evening to make her hate him—at least, to make her look frightened when his name is mentioned to her?"

"What do you think?"

"I should say murder, or something just a little short of murder—wouldn't you?"

Greenleaf looked his bewilderment.

"No," he objected. "I don't believe she'd protect him if she knew he'd killed her sister."

"Not if she knew, perhaps," Bristow pursued ruminatively. "But if she suspected, merely suspected?"

The chief did not answer this. He was clinging now to the theory of Perry's guilt. It seemed to him the easiest one to prove.

"By the way, Mr. Bristow," he suggested, wouldn't it be a good idea for us to search the yard and garden back of this house?"

"What for?"

"There's always the chance that the murderer, in running away, dropped something, even a part of the plunder. Then, too, remember the buttons."

"Yes; I see what you mean, but it's getting late now. The light's none too good—and I'm tired, chief, tired out. Suppose we let that go until tomorrow—or you do it alone."

"No; I'll wait for you tomorrow. We can do it together."

"Oh," Bristow asked, as if suddenly remembering an important item, "what kind of shoes is Perry wearing?"

"An old pair of high-topped tennis shoes—black canvas."

"Rubber soles?"

"Yes."

"I'm sorry," observed Bristow. "That's another complication. Morley wore rubbers last night. Either he or Perry might have made that footprint on the porch."

"How about Withers?" Greenleaf advanced a new idea. "He didn't tell us anything he did after seeing Campbell leave here last night."

"That's true. You'd better see him tonight. Ask him about that; and find out what time he returned to the Brevord. If you don't get it out of him tonight, you probably never will. By tomorrow, his detective, Braceway, will be on the scene, and the chances are that Withers will talk to him and not to us—that is, if he talks at all."

"Then I'll see you in the morning?"

"Yes; any time. I'll get up early. But, if you get anything out of Withers tonight, telephone me—or if your man Jenkins reports on his search for the fellow with the gold tooth."

"O. K.," agreed the chief, and swung off down the hill.

Bristow, whom he had left absorbed in thought,

turned after a few minutes and went back to the door of No. 5. Miss Kelly answered his ring.

"I'm sorry to disturb you," he said, his smile a compliment, "but there's something I'm very anxious for you to do for me. Will you clean Miss Fulton's finger nails as soon as you can? And I want you to keep everything you get as a result of that process."

"Do her nails!" The nurse was amazed.

"Yes; please. I'll explain later. And another thing: don't cut the cuticle. Don't bother with that at all. Just get what's under the nails. You'd better use merely an orange stick, I think. Will you do that for me carefully—very carefully? It's of the greatest importance."

Miss Kelly finally said she would.

He went back to his own porch and sat a long time watching the last, fading rays of the sunset.

But he was not thinking about the landscape.

"This man Withers," he was reflecting, "and his getting this detective, Braceway. Let me think. I mustn't look at these things in the light of my theories only. Too much theorizing is confusing.

"I want to get the angle of the ordinary man in the street. How would it look to him? Why, this way: either Withers is on the level and wants to do everything possible to have the murderer caught—or he's smart enough to employ Braceway in the knowledge that neither Braceway nor anybody else can get anything from him that he doesn't want to tell—I wonder."

CHAPTER VIII

THE BREATH OF SCANDAL

A TELEGRAPH messenger laboured up to the hill on his bicycle and climbed the steps to the porch of No. 5, displaying in his hand several telegrams. Two other boys had preceded him within the last hour. Friends of the Fulton family, having read of the tragedy in afternoon papers throughout the country, were wiring their messages of sympathy.

"This was no little local, isolated affair, Bristow reflected. The prominence of the victim in Washington and in the South, together with the mystery surrounding the crime, made it a matter of national interest. If he could bring the thing to a successful issue, the capture and punishment of the right man, there would be fame in it for him. The thought stimulated him.

A few minutes later Withers came up Manniston Road and went into No. 5. Soon after that Miss Kelly brought Bristow a little paper packet.

"I'm not sure I ought to do this," she said, "but, as long as the authorities have ordered it, I guess I'm safe. This is what I get as a result of 'doing' Miss Fulton's nails."

He thanked her and reassured her.

Mattie appeared at the door to tell him his supper was ready. Before he sat down at the table, he telephoned Greenleaf.

"There's something else I want you to send to Charlotte with the Perry package."

"Same sort of thing?" inquired the chief.

"Yes—Miss Fulton's."

"Wow!" barked Greenleaf over the wire. "I never thought of that."

"That's all right. I nearly forgot it myself. How will you send for it?"

The chief thought a moment.

"I'll come after it myself," he said. "I'll be up there as soon as I see Withers. I want to talk to you about the inquest. It will be held at eleven o'clock tomorrow morning."

"Come ahead," Bristow invited. "You'll have to be up here in this neighbourhood anyway if you want to see Withers. He came up to Number Five just a few minutes ago. You can catch him there."

After supper he went back to the front porch in time to see in the dusk the white uniform and cap of a trained nurse as she came down the hill. He surmised that she was one of the six nurses who lived in No. 7, the house between his and that of the murdered woman. These nurses were employed throughout the day at the big sanitarium located just over the brow of the hill at the end of Manniston Road.

Perhaps, she could tell him what he wanted to know.

"I beg your pardon," he called to her persuasively, "but may I trouble you to come up here for a moment?"

She obeyed the summons with slow, hesitant steps.

He pushed forward a chair for her and bowed.

"Unfortunately," he apologized, "I don't know your name."

She enlightened him: "Rutgers; Miss Emily Rutgers." In his turn, he told her briefly of his connection with the murder.

"I was wondering," he began, "whether you had ever heard anything unusual from Number Five."

Miss Rutgers, who was blond and too fat, had a heavy, peculiarly hoarse voice. She wanted to be certain that he had authority to "question people" about the case. He made that clear to her.

"Well, yes," she finally said. "Mrs. Withers and Miss Fulton quarreled a good deal. We girls had remarked on it. And yesterday they had an awful row. I heard some of it because it was in the middle of the day, and I had run down here from the sanitarium to fix up the laundry we'd forgotten early in the morning."

"What did you hear?"

"It was something about money. I didn't really try to listen, but I couldn't help hearing some of it, they talked so loud."

"Yes?"

"I got the idea that Miss Fulton wanted to borrow some money from Mrs. Withers for a purpose that Mrs. Withers didn't approve of. 'Well,' I heard Mrs. Withers say after Miss Fulton had almost screamed about it, 'you can't have any more. I haven't got it. That's all there is to that. I can't let you have it when I haven't got it!'

"Miss Fulton said something—I think it was about Mr. Withers or about asking him for the money.

"'You'd better not do that,' Mrs. Withers warned her. 'I tried that once, and he flew into a perfect rage. He was so worked up that he looked like a crazy man, like a man who would do anything. He looked as if he might kill me, choke me to death, anything!'"

"Did Miss Fulton answer that?"

"If she did, I didn't hear it. I just got the impression that they were both angry and mixed up in a terrific quarrel."

"Have you ever heard anything else like that at any other time?"

"Oh, we often heard them fussing. Miss Fulton did the fussing. Mrs. Withers was almost always gentle and calm. One other time I did hear Mrs. Withers say she'd lent Miss Fulton all she could afford."

"When was that?"

"Some time ago—a month or six weeks ago; maybe two months."

"Money, always money," the lame man said.

He was silent, thoughtful, for several minutes.

"I'm ever so much obliged, Miss Rutgers," he said at last. "Every bit of evidence we can get will help us—perhaps."

Miss Rutgers had risen.

"There's one other thing, Mr. Bristow," she volunteered. "There was a man hanging around Number Five last night; rather, it was early this morning."

"How do you know that?" His voice was at once urgent.

"Bessie—Miss Hardesty and I have our beds on the sleeping porch. Hers is the one nearest to Number Five. She told me about it this morning. At about one o'clock—or between one and two—she thought she heard a sloppy footstep near the sleeping porch. At that time it was raining, but not hard—just a fine drizzle.

"She went to the wiring that walls the sleeping porch on the end toward Number Five, and she made out the figure of a man coming from the front of Number Five and going toward the back fence. He had just passed the sleeping porch. She turned on the little flashlight we keep out there and saw him."

"Who was it? Could she make him out at all?"

"She said it was a negro."

"Did she see his face?"

"Not enough to recognize him, but enough to make her sure he was a black man."

"She didn't try to identify him?"

"Well, she thought it was the darky Perry who does so much work in this neighbourhood. She said she thought so because the figure of the man she saw in the rain reminded her of Perry's general appearance."

"Did she call out to him?"

"No, and he didn't run. He just walked fast and was out of sight in a moment. When I heard of the murder early this afternoon, I was up at the sanitarium, and I went to the matron and told her what I've just told you. It was her advice that, as soon as I got off duty, I should come down here and telephone what I knew to the police. She didn't want me to do it from the sanitarium because the patients might have heard it and become too much excited."

"I see. Where's Miss Hardesty now?"

"This is her night on duty at the sanitarium."

"I see. Well, she'll have to testify at the inquest tomorrow. You might tell her that. Never mind, though. The police will notify her."

"I know she won't like that much," Miss Rutgers declared; "but, of course, she's tell what she knows. How about me?"

"I can't say yet, but I don't think we'll need you at the inquest. We may need you later."

"Very well," she consented. "Let me know when the times comes. Good night, Mr. Bristow."

He went inside and picked up a novel. He wanted to "clear his brain" for the talk with the chief of police.

Greenleaf came in, looking downcast.

"What did you get from Withers?" Bristow asked.

"Nothing but a good bawling out," the chief said testily. "We won't get anything more from him for some time. He told me so. He said: 'You fellows have been carrying things with a high hand today, questioning and frightening everybody with your hidden threats and third degrees. Get out! I'll do my talking to Sam Braceway tomorrow.' But I did ask him one question—the thing you wanted to know. I asked him whether he had worn rubber shoes last night."

"What did he say?" Bristow was inwardly amused by Greenleaf's pertinacity.

"He said it was none of my business; and he flew into a rage about it—worse than he was in here this morning. He looked like a crazy man. I watched him gesticulate and get red in the face and foam and splutter. Why, he looked like a man who might commit murder any moment."

At that, Bristow started. The chief's words were strikingly like what Miss Rutgers had told him she had heard Mrs. Withers say: "He looked as if he might kill me, choke me to death, anything!"

"He's going to spend the night in Number Five," Greenleaf concluded; "he and Miss Fulton and the nurse, Miss Kelly."

Bristow tossed his novel into a vacant chair and spread out his hands.

"Well, chief," he said, "what do you make out of all this? What do you intend to do at the inquest tomorrow? By the way, here's something you'll need."

He related what Miss Rutgers had told him.

"I'm willing to take your advice," Greenleaf announced, "but this is my idea: we'll present all we have against Perry, and have him held for the grand jury. We've got enough to do that—the buttons evidence, his failure to present anything like an alibi, the mark of the rubber sole on the front porch, the inability of the woman, Lucy Thomas, to say whether or not she gave Perry the kitchen key to Number Five."

"She can't remember that, can she?"

"No; not even when we've got her locked up in jail."

"Chief, do you think Perry killed and robbed Mrs. Withers?"

"I think this," he replied: "it's an even chance he did. If he didn't, it's a sure thing that his being accused of it and locked up for it may make the real criminal more careless and give us a better chance to catch him."

"Yes; you're right. What reports have you had on the mysterious man Withers says he saw, the fellow with the long-visored cap, long raincoat, and gold tooth?"

"A little something. Jenkins has scoured the town pretty well in the time he had. A clerk at Maplewood Inn thinks—*thinks*—he saw such a man in the lobby there about three weeks ago. And one of our patrolmen, Ashurst, says he's pretty certain he saw him two months ago near here, in fact down on Freeman Avenue near where Manniston Road branches off from it. It was at night, nearly midnight."

"Did Ashurst watch him?"

"Only carelessly. Says he saw him walk on down Freeman Avenue as if he intended going into the town."

"What did the clerk see? What did this fellow do in the Maplewood Inn lobby?"

"Nothing—came in, bought a pack of cigarettes, and went out."

"Anybody else seen him?"

"Not so far as we've been able to discover."

"Has he ever registered at any of the hotels here?"

"Not that we can find; no, never."

"Funny," ruminated Bristow, "very funny. Yes, I think you're right, chief. Put up the case against Perry until we can do something better or prove it on him absolutely. Of course, if the laboratory test shows that he had human flesh—a white person's flesh—under his finger nails, that will settle it in my mind. There couldn't be any other answer."

"Will the test show whether it's a white person's skin or a nigger's?"

"Of course. There's no pigment in a white person's skin."

"Is that so? That's something I never knew before. Anyway, it certainly will nail him, won't it? But, you don't feel anyways sure Perry's the guilty man, do you?"

"No, I can't say I do. I'll tell you what we've got to consider, and it's not a very pretty theory; either that Morley killed Mrs. Withers, and Miss Fulton knows it; or that Morley and Miss Fulton together killed her; or that, although Perry killed her, we, in looking for the murderer, have come pretty near to stumbling on some sort of a nasty family scandal, something in which Maria Fulton, Enid Withers and George Withers, with perhaps another man, all have been mixed up.

"I mean a scandal ugly enough for all the rest of them to make desperate attempts to keep it hidden, even when Mrs. Withers is dead and gone. Frankly, I didn't believe Withers was in on the murder or that he believes Maria had anything to do with it or knows how it was done.

"But Maria Fulton—that's different. How else are we to explain her behaviour with us when we tried to interview her, the fact of her sudden abhorrence for Morley, the man to whom she was engaged only yesterday?

"And how else are we to explain Morley's unexplained two hours of last night, and his apparent terror today, and his whole connection with the case—the matter of the ring found in his hotel room, and all that? There's something fishy about this thing somehow, something fishy that includes Maria Fulton and Morley.

"This fellow with the brown beard and the gold tooth strengthens the theory of some rotten scandal. He must be mixed up in it some way. I'll bet anything, though, that he had nothing to do with the murder. That's what we want to get at—this inside scandal, this something which existed long before the murder but yet may have led indirectly to the murder."

Greenleaf sighed and passed his hand wearily across his eyes. He had had a hard day, the hardest day of his life.

"But you think my plan for the inquest is all right?" he asked once more.

"Yes; it's the best thing possible. By the way, don't have me summoned to testify. Leave my evidence until the trial. I don't want to wear myself out going down there for merely an inquest."

"All right; I'll fix that. We've enough evidence

without yours—enough for the inquest, anyway."

"Thanks."

Bristow looked at his watch, and Greenleaf got up to go.

"I'll be up here between eight and nine tomorrow morning," he said, "if that suits you."

"What for?"

"To get a good look at the grounds back of Number Five. If the murderer dropped anything, I want to be the man to pick it up."

"Oh, I'd forgotten that," Bristow said in a tone indicating his hopelessness of finding anything worth while. "Yes; I'll be ready for you."

Something else was on Greenleaf's mind.

"This Braceway," he said sarcastically, "the smartest detective in the South. He'll be here in the morning. What will we do? Work with him?"

"Sure," Bristow replied heartily, as if to forestall the other's dislike of the new-comer. "Even if he were no good, the best thing we could do would be to work with him. And, as he's something of a world-beater, we'll get the benefit of his ideas. By all means, let's all keep together on this thing."

"All right," Greenleaf agreed, his tone a little surly. "Your appointment to my force is O. K. I fixed that this afternoon. Good night."

"Good night—and don't forget to send that stuff off to the Charlotte laboratory tonight. If we can find out who scratched somebody last night, if we can determine who had little bits of foreign skin under the finger nails today, we've got the answer to this murder mystery. That's one thing sure."

Bristow turned off the lights in the living room

and went to his dressing room to prepare for bed on the sleeping porch.

"Money," he was thinking as he undressed; "money and fifteen thousand dollars' worth of jewelry. Where has it all gone? That's the thing that will settle this case, and I think—I think I've a pretty good idea of what will be proved about it."

CHAPTER IX

WOMEN'S NERVES

LUCY THOMAS in a cell in the Furmville jail sat on the edge of her cot at midnight, staring into inky darkness while she tried to remember the events of the night before. She was not of the slow-witted, stupid-looking type of negro women. The thing against which she struggled was not poverty of brain but the mist of forgetfulness with which the fumes of liquor had surrounded her.

Questioned and requestioned by the police during the afternoon and early evening, she had been able to tell them only that she and Perry had been drinking together in her little two-room cabin. When he had left her, what he had said, whether he had returned—these points were as effectually covered up in her mind as if she had never had cognizance of them.

She did remember, however, certain things which she had not imparted to the police. One was that at some time during the night there had been a struggle between herself and Perry. The other was that at some time, far into the night or very early in the morning, she had heard the clank-clank of the iron key falling on the floor of her house, a key which she had worn suspended on a ribbon round her neck.

She rocked herself back and forth on the cot, her head throbbing, her mouth parched, tears in her eyes. To the white people, she thought, it did not matter much, but to her the fact that she and Perry had intended to get married was the biggest thing in her life.

"I don't know; I don't know," her thoughts ran bitterly. "Ef Perry tuk dat key away fum me, he mus' done gawn to dat house—an' he wuz full uv likker. Ef he ain' done tuk dat key fum me an' den later flung it back on de flo' uv my house, who did do it?"

She sobbed afresh.

"He is one mean nigger when he gits too much likker in him. Ain' nobody knows dat better'n I does. An' he sayed somethin' las' night 'bout gittin' a whole lot uv money. He—"

She moaned and flung herself backward on the cot.

"Gawd have mussy! Gawd have mussy! I done remembuhed. I done remembuhed. He done say somethin' 'bout dat white woman's gol' an' jewelery. Gawd! Dat's whut he done. He done it! Dat's why he wuz fightin' me. He wuz tryin' to git dat kitchen key. An' he got it! He got it! Ef he done kilt dat woman, de white folks goin' to git him sho'ly—sho'ly. An' him an' me ain' nevuh gwine git married—nevuh. Dey'll kill him or dey'll sen' him to dat pen. Aw, my Gawd! My Gawd!"

She sat up again and began to think about Mrs. Withers, how well the slain woman had treated her, how kindly. From that, her thoughts went to ghosts. She fell to trembling and moaning in an audible key. It was not long before a warden, awakened by her cries of terror, had to visit her and threaten bodily punishment if she did not keep quiet.

After a while, she relapsed into her quiet sobbing.

"I think maybe he done tuk dat key. I knows he done lef' me durin' de night, an' I b'lieve he done come back. But I ain't gwine say nothin'. Maybe I don' know. Maybe I is mistuk. De whole thing done got too mix' up fuh me. Maybe he kilt her an' maybe he ain' been nigh de place. But I wish I coul' know. My holy Lawd! I wish I done know all dat done happen.

"Dat key fallin' on de flo'. Who done drap it dar ef Perry ain' drapped it? Dat's whut I'd like to know. Ef he ain' had dat key, ain' nobody had it."

She lay down, weeping and sobbing from unhappiness and terror. Bristow and Greenleaf would have given much to have known her suspicions, suspicions which amounted to a moral certainty.

On the sleeping porch of No. 5, Manniston Road, Maria Fulton lay awake a long time and tortured herself by reviewing again and again the thoughts that had crushed her during the day. Miss Kelly, on a cot at the foot of the girl's bed, heard her stirring restlessly but could not know in the darkness how her long, slender fingers tore at the bed-covering, nor how her face was drawn with pain.

"The overturning of that chair,"—her mind whirled the events before her—"the sound of that whisper, that man's whisper, and the sight of that foot! He wore rubbers. I know he did. He always wears them when it's even cloudy. It was he! It was he!"

Her nails dug into her palms as she fought for something like self-control.

"If it was not he, I would never have fainted—never. That's what made me faint, the sickening, undeniable knowledge that that was who it was. And I loved him! But—but the rubber-shod foot, the size of it! Am I sure? Could it have been——"

She groaned so that Miss Kelly lifted her head from her own pillow and listened intently, trying to determine whether the sufferer was asleep or awake.

"He's not stupid," she swept on, closing mutinous lips against the repetition of sound. "He knew Enid could do nothing—nothing more. I don't understand. Oh, I don't understand! I wonder now why I said I heard nothing.

"I wonder why I lay unconscious on the floor near the dining room door all those hours—until ten o'clock this morning. It was because the knowledge was too much for me to stand—just as it is too much now. And I can't share it with anybody. I'll never be able to get it off my conscience. If I did, they'd hang him—or the other one who——"

At that thought, she screamed aloud, a wild, eerie sound that chilled the blood of even Miss Kelly, accustomed as she was to the cries of suffering and despair. The nurse was at the hysterical girl's side in a moment, holding her quivering body in strong, capable arms.

"What was it? What was it, Miss Fulton?" she asked soothingly.

Maria brushed the back of her hand across her forehead, which was beaded with big, cold drops of perspiration.

"Nothing, Miss Kelly; nothing," she half-moaned. "A bad dream, a nightmare, I guess. Give me something to make me sleep."

She drank eagerly from a glass the nurse put to her lips.

"If I begin to talk in my sleep, Miss Kelly, call me, wake me up, will you?" she begged, the fright still in her voice.

"Yes, I will." This reassuringly while Miss Kelly smoothed the pillows and readjusted the tumbled coverings.

Maria grasped her arm in a grip that hurt.

"But will you?" she demanded sharply. "Promise me!"

"Yes; indeed, I will. I promise."

Miss Kelly meant what she said. She was not anxious to be the recipient of the sick girl's confidences.

CHAPTER X

EYES OF ACCUSATION

BRISTOW, at his early breakfast, devoted himself, between mouthfuls, to the front page of *The Furmville Sentinel.* It was given up entirely to the Withers murder.

" Murder—murder horrible and mysterious—was committed early yesterday morning," announced the paper in large black-face type, " when the beautiful and charming Mrs. Enid Fulton Withers, wife of George S. Withers, the well-known attorney of Atlanta, was choked to death in the parlour of her home at No. 5 Manniston Road. The most heinous crime that has ever stained the annals of Furmville," etc.

The article went on to recite that Chief Greenleaf of the Furmville police force had been fortunate in securing the assistance of a genius in running down the various clues that seemed to point to the guilty party. Mr. Lawrence Bristow, of Cincinnati, now in town for his health, had worked with him all day in unearthing many circumstances " which, although each of them seemed trivial, led when summed up to the almost irrefutable conviction that the murder was done by a drunken negro, Perry Carpenter," etc.

In spite of this, the paper continued, the dead woman's husband, arriving unexpectedly on the scene, had employed by wire Samuel S. Braceway, the professional detective of Atlanta, who would reach Furmville early this morning and, probably, work with Chief Greenleaf, Mr. Bristow, and the plain-clothes squad in the effort to remove all doubts of the guilt of the accused negro.

There followed a sketch of Braceway which was enough to convince the readers that in him Mr. Withers had called into the case the shrewdest man in the South, "very probably the shrewdest man in the entire country."

"Evidently," Bristow was thinking when Greenleaf rang the door-bell, "while I'm a 'genius,' Braceway's the man everybody relies on when it comes to catching the murderer."

The chief was in a hurry, and the two men, going out of Bristow's back door, walked down to the corner of the sleeping porch of No. 7, the nurses' home. The frail wire fences that had served to partition the back lots of Nos. 5, 7, and 9 had either fallen down or been carried away, but there was a tall five-board fence at the rear of the three lots. From this board fence, the hill sloped down toward the southeast, the direction in which the negro settlement containing the home of Lucy Thomas was located.

Bristow, frankly bored by the belated search, let Greenleaf lead the way.

"I went up to the sanitarium late last night," the chief told him, "and had a long talk with Miss Hardesty. She says the man she saw night before last was right here, just a few yards from this Number Seven sleeping porch; and, it seemed to her, he made straight for the board fence. We'll follow in his footsteps. That will take up to the fence in the middle of the rear line of Number Seven's lot."

He was following this route as he talked, Bristow limping a few yards behind him.

Greenleaf overlooked nothing. The lot had been cleared of last winter's leaves, and the search was comparatively simple, but, if he saw even so much as a small stick on either side of him, he turned it over. They were soon at the fence, about twenty yards from the sleeping porch.

"There's not a trace—not a trace of anything, chief," said Bristow, leaning one elbow on the top board of the fence.

Greenleaf, however, was not to be discouraged. After he had walked around again and again in ever-widening circles, he stopped and thought.

"If that nigger was running away and trying to make good time," he exclaimed, suddenly inspired, "he didn't jump the fence in the middle there, where you are. He took a line slanting down toward that negro settlement. The chances are he went over the fence down at that corner."

He pointed to the southeastern corner back of No. 5 and, with his eyes on the ground, began to work toward it.

Barely a yard from the corner, he stooped down swiftly, picked up something and turned joyfully toward Bristow, who still leaned against the fence.

"Look here! Look here, Mr. Bristow," he called, hurrying across to him.

Bristow examined the object Greenleaf had found. It consisted of six links of a gold chain, three of the links very small and of plain gold, the other alternating three links being larger and chased with a fine, exquisite design of laurel leaves, the leaves so small as to be barely distinguishable to the naked eye.

The lame man shared the chief's excitement.

" By George! You've got something worth while. I should say so!"

" What do you make of it? asked Greenleaf, eager and pleased. " It must have belonged to Mrs. Withers, don't you think?"

" There's one way to find out," Bristow answered, looking at his watch. It was half-past eight o'clock. " Let's go and ask Withers."

They went around to the front of No. 5.

" One of the end links is broken," Bristow said as they ascended the steps. " My guess it that this is a part of the necklace Mrs. Withers wore when she was killed. You remember the mark on the back of her neck. It might have been made by the jerk that would have been required to break these links."

Miss Kelly, answering their ring, told them Mr. Withers had gone to the railroad station to meet Mr. Braceway.

" Then, too," she added, " Miss Fulton's father is due on the nine o'clock train. Mr. Withers may stop down town to meet him."

" I'd forgotten about that," said Bristow. " We'll have to ask your help." He handed her the fragment of chain. " Will you be so kind as to take that back to Miss Fulton and ask her whether she recognizes it, whether she can identify it?"

Miss Kelly complied with the request at once. She returned in a few moments.

"Miss Fulton," she reported, handing the links back to Bristow, "says this is a part of the chain Mrs. Withers wore round her neck night before last. She wore a lavalliere; it had two emeralds and eighteen rather small diamonds."

"Good!" exclaimed Greenleaf, glancing at the lame man. "I guess that fixes Perry."

"Undoubtedly," Bristow assented; and spoke to Miss Kelly: "I beg your pardon, but is Miss Fulton up this morning, or will she be up later?"

"She's dressing now. She wants to be up to meet her father."

"In that case, I'll wait until later. What I would like to have is a complete, detailed description of all of Mrs. Withers' jewelry. I wish you'd mention that to her, will you?"

Greenleaf was anxious to return to his office.

"This last piece of evidence," he said, "ought to go to the coroner's jury. It clinches the case against Perry. Here's the whole business in a nutshell: the buttons missing from his blouse, one found in Number Five, the other in your bungalow; Miss Hardesty's having seen him the night of the murder; the ease with which he undoubtedly got the kitchen key from Lucy Thomas; the imprint of his rubber-soled shoe on the porch; the finding of this piece of gold chain; and his failure to establish an alibi. It's more than enough to have him held for the grand jury—it's murder in the first degree."

Bristow went back to his porch. Looking down to his left and through the trees, he commanded a view of Freeman Avenue.

"When I see an automobile flash past that spot," he decided, "I'll hurry down to Number Five. I want to be there to witness the meeting between Miss Fulton and her father. It may be possible that, when this scandal—whatever it was—was about to break concerning Mrs. Withers, this family was lucky enough to have a negro hauled up as the murderer. In any event, it's up to me to keep track of the relations between Fulton, his daughter, Withers, and Morley. The psychology of the situation now is as important as any material evidence."

He did not have long to wait. At a quarter past nine he caught a glimpse of a big car speeding out Freeman Avenue. He sprang to his feet, hurried down to No. 5, rang the bell, and was inside the living room by the time the machine had climbed up Manniston Road and deposited in front of the door its one passenger. He was a man of sixty-five or sixty-seven years of age, very white of hair, very erect of figure.

Bristow did not have time or need to formulate an excuse for his presence before Mr. Fulton rushed up the steps to meet Maria. As she came from the direction of the bedrooms to greet him, her expression had in it reluctance, timidity even.

The father and daughter met in the centre of the

living room. Bristow, stationed near the corner by the door, could see their faces. He watched them with attention strained to the utmost.

In the eyes of Maria there was a great fear mingled with a look of pleading. The old man's face was deep-lined; under his eyes were dark pouches; and his lips were tightly compressed, as if he sought to prevent his bursting into condemnation.

With a little catch in her voice, Maria cried out, "Father!" and stood watching him.

For a moment the old man's eyes were dreary with accusation. Bristow had never seen an emotion mirrored so clearly, so indisputably, in anybody's eyes. It was a speaking, thundering light, he thought.

The father, without opening his mouth, plainly said to the girl:

"At last, you've killed her! It's all your fault. You've killed her."

Bristow read that as easily as if it had been held before him in printed words. So, apparently, did Miss Fulton. The pleading expression left her face, and, in place of it, was only a flourishing, lively fear.

But Fulton put out his arms and gathered her into them, took hold of her mechanically, displaying neither fondness nor a desire to comfort and soothe.

Bristow quietly left the room and returned to his porch.

"Her father," he analyzed what he had seen, "blames her for the tragedy—possibly believes her guilty of the actual murder. Why? This is a new angle—brand new."

He went in and called up Greenleaf, only to be told that the chief had left word he was to be found at the Brevord Hotel. Telephoning there, he got him on the wire.

"Neither Withers nor Braceway came up here with old Mr. Fulton," he began.

"I know," put in the chief. "I'm down here to meet Braceway now. He and Withers are in conference. Braceway doesn't want to go to the inquest. I'm to take him by the undertaker's to look at the body, and then he wants to run up to see you. Says he won't learn anything important at the inquest; he'd rather talk to you."

"All right," returned Bristow. "That suits me perfectly. When will he be here?"

"In half an hour, I suppose. And I'll run up as soon as the inquest is over."

"I wonder," Bristow communed again with himself, "whether this Braceway is on the level, whether Withers is on the level. What's their game—to find the real murderer or to shut up a family scandal?"

The scandal theory bothered him. He saw no way of getting at it.

In less than an hour he and Braceway were shaking hands on the porch of No. 9. Bristow, studying him rapidly, motioned him to a chair.

Here was no ordinary police-detective type. This man had neither square-toed shoes, nor a bull neck, nor coarseness of feature. About thirty-six years old, he was unusually slender, and straight as a dart, a peculiar and restless gracefulness characterizing all his movements. He seemed fairly to exude energy. He was keyed up to lightning-like motion. He gave the impression of having a brain that worked with the precision and force of some great machine, a machine that never missed fire.

From the toes of his highly polished tan shoes to the sheen of his blond hair and the crown of his nobby straw hat, he looked like a well dressed and prosperous professional man. His dark gray suit with a thin thread of pale green in it, his silver-gray necktie, the gloves he carried in his left hand, every detail of his appearance marked him, first as a "snappy dresser," and second as a highly efficient man.

While they exchanged casual greetings, Braceway lit a cigarette and spun the match, with a droning sound, far out from the porch. He did this, as he did everything else, with a "flaire," with that indefinable something which marks every man who has a strong personality. There was in all his bearing a dash, an electric emphasis.

"What do you think, Mr. Bristow?" He got down to business at once. "Did this negro Perry kill Mrs. Withers?"

Braceway blew out a big cloud of smoke and looked intently at his new acquaintance.

"I've talked to Greenleaf," he supplemented. "I suppose he gave me all the facts you've collected. But Greenleaf—you know what I mean," he waved his cigarette hand expressively; "I wouldn't say he had extraordinary powers of divination. He's a good fellow, and all that, but—what do you think?"

"On the evidence alone, so far," Bristow answered with an appreciative, warming smile, "I'd say Perry committed the crime."

"Oh; yes, sure." He moved quickly in his chair. "On the evidence, but there are other things, other factors. What do you think?"

"I'm afraid that's my trouble," Bristow told him. "I've been thinking so much that I'm somewhat muddled. But I believe there may be something more than a negro's greed back of this thing."

"Now you're speaking mouthfuls," Braceway said, smiling brightly. "Tell me about it."

Bristow told him—about Withers' peculiar behaviour; the whole case against Perry; the illusive personage with the chestnut beard and gold tooth; Morley's suspicious story and actions; and, lastly, Maria Fulton's highly puzzling narrative of what she had seen and not seen in connection with the murder.

Braceway listened with complete absorption, in a way that showed he was photographing each incident and statement on his brain.

"Now," he began with almost explosive suddenness, "let's get this straight. I want to work with you, if you'll let me." He paused long enough for Bristow to nod a pleased assent. "And I believe there's something back of this crime that nobody has yet put his finger on. Mr. Withers believes it. Don't make any mistake about that. Withers is as anxious to get the real criminal as you and I are."

"Let me understand," Bristow said in his turn.

"Do you propose that we work on the case with the supposition that Withers is in no way responsible for any part of the tragedy?"

"Absolutely!" snapped out Braceway, thoroughly good natured despite his abruptness. "At least, that's my plan. I'm certain Withers had nothing to do with it."

For the first time, something far back in Bristow's brain stirred uneasily, as if, miles away, somebody had sounded an alarm. Should he trust this man? Would Braceway try to pick up a false scent, try to throw the whole thing out of gear?

Although he, Bristow, had expressed to Greenleaf only last night his confidence in Withers' innocence, would it be wise to hold to such a belief? The future was too uncertain, too apt to produce entirely unexpected things. At any rate, it would be silly to call himself anything of a criminologist and yet go ahead with a blind, spoken conviction of the innocence of a man who unquestionably had acted in a way to bring suspicion upon himself.

He would wait and see. He purposed to throw away no card that might later take a trick.

"Very good," he said. "That suits me if you're satisfied. You can answer for him, I don't doubt."

"Thoroughly so. In the first place, he and I are close personal friends; went to college together; were fraternity mates; had an office together until I quit practising law and went in for this sort of work. Then, too, I've turned him inside out this morning. He doesn't know a thing.

"And, I might as well tell you now, he didn't hang around Manniston Road night before last after his wife got in. As soon as he saw this Douglas Campbell go home he returned to the Brevord and went to bed.

"No, sirree! Here's what I work on: either Morley killed her, or the negro killed her, or it was done by the mysterious fellow with the gold tooth. How does that strike you?"

"Correctly; I'm with you," agreed Bristow, still with the mental reservation that he would deal with Withers as he saw fit.

"One thing more," added Braceway, and Bristow was surprised to see that he looked a trifle embarrassed; "I want you to handle all the talk that has to be had with Miss Maria Fulton. I'll be frank with you; I have to be. It's this way: I was once in love with her; in fact, engaged to marry her. Do you see?"

"Fully."

He was glad to know at the outset that Braceway was a friend of the family. It might be valuable later.

Braceway threw away his cigarette and sighed with relief.

"I'm glad you understand," he said. "Now, about Withers: things have begun to happen to him already—this morning. Since this has hit him, he doesn't know where he'll get off eventually. I'll tell you."

CHAPTER XI

THE $1,000 CHECK .

A FEW minutes after eight o'clock that morning Mr. Illington, president of the Furmville National Bank, had called at the Brevord to see Mr. Withers, who, still holding his room there, was waiting for the delayed morning. train.

Mr. Illington was of the true banker type, fifty years old, immaculately dressed, thin of lip, hard of eye, slow and precise in his enunciation. He had, apparently, estranged himself from any deep, human feeling. The long handling of money had hardened him. His fingers were long and grasping, and his voice was quite as metallic as the clink of gold coins one upon the other.

At Mr. Withers' invitation he took a chair in Mr. Withers' room. He rubbed his dry, slender hands together and cleared his throat, after which he spoke his little set speech of condolence.

Mr. Withers, haggard from grief and lack of sleep, waved aside these preliminary remarks.

The banker put his hand into his breast pocket and drew forth a bulky envelope, from which he produced a long, rectangular piece of paper.

" I knew you would prefer to learn of this at first hand from the bank; indeed, from me, its president. Yesterday, Mr. Withers, a promissory note, a sixty-day note, for a thousand dollars fell due in the Furmville National Bank. You might like to see it. Here it is."

He handed the piece of paper to Withers, who saw that the note had been signed by Maria Fulton and endorsed by Enid Fulton Withers. The husband of the dead woman was too astonished to comment.

"We acted as—as leniently in the matter as we could, perhaps more leniently than was strictly proper in banking circles," Mr. Illington was pleased to explain. "I myself called up Miss Fulton on the telephone yesterday, but naturally she was so agitated that she seemed unable to give me any information as to what she intended to do regarding the—er—liquidation of this indebtedness."

"And," concluded Withers, passing the note back to him, "since my wife was the endorser, it's up to me to make the note good, to pay the bank the thousand dollars."

Mr. Illington was glad to see how thoroughly the bereaved husband appreciated the situation.

"Quite right, entirely so," he said. "And will you?"

"Of course."

"Ahem—When?" inquired the banker, assuming an expression of casual interest.

"I haven't that much money on deposit in Atlanta, but I can get it. I return to Atlanta this afternoon. I can send the money to you tomorrow. Will that answer?"

"Oh, perfectly, perfectly," assented Mr. Illington, much reassured. "We are always glad, at the Furmville National, to do the reasonable and accommodating thing. Yes; that will be thoroughly satisfactory.—Ahem! I have a new note here. You might sign it? To keep things regular, in order."

Withers signed the new note. It was for five days.

Illington got to his feet with stiff dignity.

"Glad to accommodate you, Mr. Withers; very glad. I wish you good morning," he concluded, going toward the door.

"Good-bye," replied Withers absently, but looked up suddenly. "By the way, I might like to know something about the disposition of that thousand dollars. Could you tell me anything concerning it?"

Mr. Illington came back to his chair and reseated himself, again producing the bulky envelope.

"I was prepared for just such a request, a perfectly natural request," he answered Withers' question, plainly approving of his own forehandedness.

He took from the envelope and passed to Withers a canceled check.

"This," he said, "gives you the information you desire. You see, I gathered from the newspaper reports this morning and from the gossip of the street yesterday afternoon that there might be more or less of—er—a mystery in this—ah—distressing situation. Consequently, I brought along this check which, curiously enough, had not been called for by the maker of it."

Withers, disregarding the banker's remarks, was studying the check. It had been signed by Enid

Fulton Withers, to whom the $1,000 loan had evidently been credited at the Furmville National. It was for $1,000, and it was made payable to Maria Fulton. Maria Fulton had indorsed it, and, below her endorsement, appeared that of Henry Morley, showing that the money had passed directly into the hands of Morley.

"That's all I wanted to know," Withers said quietly, giving the check back to Illington. "I'm much obliged."

This time Illington departed, taking himself off with a feeling of having done his duty with promptitude and according to the best business ethics.

His visit had prevented Withers' meeting the train, and Fulton had gone directly to Manniston Road.

Braceway, going to the hotel on the banker's heels, was admitted by Withers, who broke into a storm of futile, highly coloured profanity.

"Brace," he said, "you'll get the devil who's caused all this, won't you? You know what my life has been! You'll get him if you have to tear up heaven and earth."

"Sure! Sure!" Braceway declared. "Keep yourself together. Let me do the worrying. I'll get him if he's above the sod."

"So, you see," Braceway said, in reciting the incident to Bristow, "we're getting a little warm on the scent. This Morley, this wooer of Maria, seems to have his head within stinging range of the hornets, doesn't he?"

"Undoubtedly."

"What do you make of it?" pressed Braceway.

Bristow thought a little while.

"It might be this," he advanced: "Morley is in trouble with his bank, short in his accounts—probably has been for several months. Two months ago, sixty-one days ago, he confided to Miss Fulton that he stood in great danger of arrest, pointed out that he had made a mistake, asked assistance from her, told her a thousand dollars would arrange things.

"But, instead of paying the thousand into the bank, he went to gambling with it in the hope of trebling or quadrupling it and—lost it. In other words, he's been afraid to tell his financée how much he really owed the bank and then played the thousand to win enough to enable him to square himself."

"Once more," observed the Atlanta man, "you speak in mouthfuls."

"Again and further—of course, all this is on the theory that Morley is a pusillanimous kind of man; but he would have to be just that to be taking money from a woman, any woman, much less the one to whom he is engaged to be married—again and further, when he had lost the thousand and saw ruin just ahead of him again, he ran down here and asked for more money.

"Perhaps, Mrs. Withers, at her sister's tearful request, had previously raised more than a thousand for him, had added to that thousand other money obtained from pawning some of her jewelry; and he now insisted that Maria make Mrs. Withers go the limit and pawn *all* her jewelry.

"By George!" Bristow concluded. "That may explain the quarrel which Miss Rutgers, the trained nurse in Number Seven, heard the two sisters engaged in the day before the murder. Yes; it might. Evidently, Mrs. Withers refused to be bled further. After that, what? What would you say?"

"It's plain enough," Braceway answered. "There was Morley, crazed by the fear of arrest and conviction for embezzlement. There was Mrs. Withers, still possessing and holding enough jewelry to get him out of trouble, if he had time to convert the jewels into cash and to get back to his bank with the money.

"What was the result of that situation? Evidently, he never intended to catch that midnight train. He did what he had planned to do, came back to Number Five, confronted Mrs. Withers soon after her escort had left her at the door, demanded the jewels, was refused; and then, in a blind rage or a panic, killed her and stole the jewels."

"There's no use blinking the fact," said Bristow in a quiet, calculating way, trying to keep in his mind all the other peculiar circumstances surrounding this crime. "From the way we've put it, the thing reads as plainly as a primer. Now, what are we to do? Even now, we haven't the proof on him —any real proof."

"Suppose," said Braceway, "we let him leave Furmville, let him go back to Washington, with the hope that he does pawn the stuff he's stolen?"

"And suppose," Bristow added, "we get a detailed description of all the jewelry Mrs. Withers owned, and wire that description to the police of the principal towns between here and Washington and between here and Atlanta. We'll make the request, of course, that they watch the pawnshops and nab anybody who shows up with any of the Withers stuff?"

"That's it! That's it as sure as you're born!" Braceway struck the arm of his chair and catapulted himself into a standing position. "That will get him—provided, of course, he's desperate enough to take the chance of pawning any of it."

"One other thing," Bristow supplemented. "You said Withers said something to you this morning about your knowing what his life had been. Just what did he mean?"

Braceway reflècted a moment.

"There's no reason for your not knowing it," he confided. "Withers had rather a trying life with his wife. It was a baffling sort of a situation. She was in love with him. I haven't a doubt of that. And he was in love with her.

"She was one of the most fascinating women I ever saw. They used to say in Atlanta that all the women liked her, and that any man who had once shaken hands with her and looked her in the eye was, forever after, her obedient servant.

"But she was never entirely frank with Withers. Naturally, that at first made him regretful, and later it made him jealous. You know his type. I'm not sure that I have the whole story, but that's the foundation of it, and it led to bitter disagreements and fierce quarrels.

"Some of their acquaintances got on to it, and

couldn't understand why a woman like her and a good fellow like Withers couldn't hit it off. Things got worse and worse. I don't believe Withers minded her being up here with her sister. The temporary separation came, probably, as a great relief to both of them."

"I see," Bristow said. "Naturally, when, on top of all that, the money began to fly and the jewels went into pawn, he came to the end of his rope—determined to put a stop to the thing."

"Probably," said Braceway, looking at his watch. "But how about our little job—getting the description of the jewelry and having Greenleaf wire it out? I'll go down to Number Five and get it from Withers and his father-in-law."

"You don't mind seeing Miss Fulton?" Bristow asked interestedly.

"Oh, no," he answered, embarrassment again in his manner. "But I don't feel like cross-questioning her. You can understand that. You'll have to take on that end, really."

Bristow thought: "He's still in love with her. I was right about her. There's a lot to her if she can hold a live wire like this." Aloud he said:

"All right. You get the list. In the meantime, I'll telephone Greenleaf to tell Morley he can go to Washington tomorrow if he wants to—but not today."

"Why not today?"

"Because there are some things here you and I had better go over, and I think we'd do well to follow Morley, don't you? That is, if we want to get the goods on him without fail."

"Now that I think of it, yes. Perhaps, both of us needn't go, but one will have to."

He went down the steps, saying Withers had by this time arrived at No. 5 and would be waiting there with Mr. Fulton. Both the father and the husband would accompany the body of Mrs. Withers to Atlanta on the four o'clock train that afternoon.

Bristow, having caught Greenleaf by telephone at the inquest, gave him their decision about Morley's departure the next day, and announced that he and Braceway would like him to send out by wire the description of the Withers jewels. To both of these propositions Greenleaf agreed. Bristow returned to his porch.

"So," he thought, "it's got to be Morley or the negro."

And yet, he decided, in spite of the theorizing he and Braceway had indulged in, there was small chance now of fixing the crime definitely on Morley. He had none of the jewelry, apparently. The police had searched his baggage and his room at the hotel, without success. Indubitably, it would be more likely that a jury would convict Perry. All the direct evidence was against the negro.

Bristow did not deceive himself. It would be a great satisfaction and a morsel to his vanity to prove the negro guilty. He foresaw that the papers sooner or later would get hold of the fact that Braceway was after Morley.

And, although they had hinted at mystery and uncertainty this morning, they had printed their stories so as to show that Greenleaf, backed by

Bristow, would try to get Perry. The duel between himself and Braceway was on. He remembered he had discounted at the beginning the idea of the negro's guilt, but that had been before the discovery of the fragment of the lavalliere chain.

Now, he was disposed, determined even, to treat everything as if Perry were the guilty man. He would work with that idea always in mind. In the meantime he would go with Braceway as long as the Braceway theories seemed to have any foundation at all. He did not want to run the risk of being shown up as a bungler. He was anxious to be "in on" anything that might happen.

"So," he concluded, "if Perry is finally convicted, I get the credit. If Morley is sent up, I'll get some of the credit for that also. I won't lose either way.

"Now, about Withers? I've got to handle him by myself. If I were analyzing this case from the newspaper accounts of it, I'd say at first blush that either Withers did the thing or Perry did it. That's what the public's saying now.

"But Braceway stands as a fence between Withers and me. He's a friend of Withers and in love with Withers' sister-in-law. And he believes Withers innocent. That's patent. For the present, I can't do anything in that direction. I've got to dig up everything possible on Morley and the negro—and, in spite of the check business, the chances are against the negro."

He called to Mattie whom he heard moving about in the dining room.

"Lucy Thomas," he said, "is out of jail now. I

wish you'd go look for her right away. The inquest is over by this time, and she'll be at home by the time you get there. Bring her back here with you. Tell her it's by order of the police, and I only want to talk to her a few minutes."

"Yas, suh," said Mattie.

"I'm not going to hurt her, Mattie," he said. "Be sure to tell her so."

"Yas, suh, Mistuh Bristow; I sho' will tell her. I 'spec' dat po' nigger is done had de bre'f skeered outen her already."

His eye was caught by the figures of Braceway and Mr. Fulton leaving No. 5. They turned and started up the walk toward No. 9.

"Mr. Fulton," Braceway explained, after the introduction to Bristow, "wants to tell you something about his—about Mrs. Withers. It brings in further complications—hard ones for us."

CHAPTER XII

THE MAN WITH THE GOLD TOOTH

MR. FULTON'S arms trembled as he put his hands on the arms of a chair and seated himself with the deliberateness of his years. In his face the lines were still deep, and once or twice his mouth twisted as if with actual pain, but there was in his eyes the flame of an indomitable will. He was by no means a crushed and weak old man. Neither the terrific blow of his daughter's death nor the reverses he had suffered in his business affairs had broken him.

"What I have to say," he began, looking first at Braceway and then at Bristow, "is not a pleasant story, but it has to be told."

His low-pitched, modulated voice was clear and without a tremor. His glance at the two men gave them the impression that he paid them a certain tribute.

"Both of you," he continued, "are gentlemen. Mr. Braceway, you're a personal friend of my son-in-law. Mr. Bristow, I know you will respect my confidence, in so far as it can be respected."

They both bowed assent. At the same moment the telephone rang. Bristow excused himself and answered it. The chief of police was on the wire.

"It's all over!" his voice sounded jubilantly. "It's all over, and I want you to congratulate me, congratulate me and yourself. It was quick work."

"What do you mean?" queried Bristow.

"The inquest is over. The coroner's jury found that Mrs. Withers came to her death at the hands of Perry Carpenter."

"And you're satisfied?"

"Sure, I'm satisfied! We've found the guilty man, and he's under lock and key. What more do I want? I'll tell you what, I'll be up to have dinner with you in a little while. I invite myself," this with a chuckle. "You and I will have a little celebration dinner. It is a go?"

"By all means. I'll be delighted to have you, and I want to hear all about the inquest."

Bristow went back to the porch.

"That," he told them, "was a message from the chief of police. He says the coroner's jury has held the negro, Perry Carpenter, for the crime."

Mr. Fulton moved forward in his chair, his hands clutching the arms of it tightly.

"I'll never believe it, never!" he declared, evidently indignant. "Nothing will ever persuade me that Enid, Mrs. Withers, met her death at the hands of an ordinary negro burglar."

"What makes you so positive of that?" Bristow asked curiously.

"Because of what has happened in the past," Fulton replied with emphasis. "I was about to tell you. This man none of you have been able to find, this man with the gold tooth, has been in Enid's life for a good many years. I don't understand why you haven't found him; I really don't."

"We haven't had two whole days to work on this

case yet," Bristow reminded him politely. "Many developments may arise."

"I hope so; I hope so," he said sharply. "That man must be found."

"One moment," Braceway put in with characteristic quickness; "how do you know he's been in your daughter's life, Mr. Fulton?"

"That goes back to the beginning of my story." He looked out across the trees and roofs of the town toward the mountains.

"Enid was always my favourite daughter. I suppose it's a mistake to distinguish between one's children, to favour one beyond the other. But she was just that—my favourite daughter—always. She had a dash, a spirit, a joyous soul. Years ago I saw that she would develop into a fascinating womanhood.

"Nothing disturbed me until she was nineteen. Then she fell in love. It was while she was spending a summer at Hot Springs, Virginia. The trouble was not in her falling in love. It was that she never told me the name of the man she loved." He leaned back again and sighed. "She never did tell me. I never knew.

"I never knew, because, when she was twenty, she came to me with the unexpected announcement that she was going to marry George Withers. I was surprised. She was not the kind to change in her likes and dislikes. And I knew Withers was not the man she had originally loved. Nevertheless, I asked her no questions, and she was married to Withers when she was barely twenty-one.

"A year later, approximately four years ago, she

and my other daughter, Maria, spent six weeks at Atlantic City in the early spring. It was there that she got into trouble. I could detect it in her letters. Some tremendous sorrow or diffculty had overtaken her, and she was fighting it alone.

"Her husband was not with her. I wrote to Maria asking her to investigate quietly, to report to me whether there was anything I could do.

"Maria's report was unsatisfactory. She knew Enid was distressed and was giving away or risking in some manner large amounts of money—even pawning her jewelry, jewelry which I had given her and which she prized above everything else. The whole thing was a mystery, Maria wrote. The very next mail I received a letter from Enid asking me to lend her two thousand dollars.

"She made no pretence of explaining why she wanted it. She didn't have to explain. I was a rich man at that time, comparatively speaking, and she knew I would give her the money.

"I mailed her a check for two thousand, but on the train which carried the check I sent a private detective—not to make any arrests, you understand, not to raise any row or start any scandal. I merely wanted to find out what or who troubled her. Women, you know, particularly good women, are prone to fall into the hands of unscrupulous people.

"Four days later the detective reported to me, but it was of no special value. He couldn't tell me where the two thousand had gone. If Enid had paid it to a man or a woman, the fellow had missed seeing the transaction. With the description of the jewels I had given him, however, he made a round of the pawnshops in Atlantic City and learned that all of them had been pawned—for a total of seven thousand."

"Pawned by whom—herself?" asked Bristow.

"No. They were pawned in different shops by a man with a gold tooth and a thick, chestnut-brown beard."

"No wonder you doubt the negro's guilt!" exclaimed Braceway.

"Excuse me," put in Bristow quickly, "but did you ever mention this to Mr. Withers?"

"Certainly, not," Fulton answered. "I never told it to a living soul. And as my inquiries had netted me practically nothing, I was obliged to let the matter drop. It was bad enough for me to have interfered with her, my daughter and a married woman, in the hope of helping her. Most assuredly, I could not have distressed her, degraded her, by telling her a detective had been investigating her."

"And that was the end of it?" asked Braceway.

"Not quite. She went back to Atlanta. Withers wanted to know where her jewels were. She wrote to me in an agony of fear and sorrow, asking me to redeem the jewels. I did it. I went to Atlantic City myself. She had sent me the tickets. It cost me seven thousand dollars."

"That was four years ago?" Braceway continued the inquiry.

"Yes."

"Did Miss Maria Fulton at that time know Henry Morley?"

"No; I think not. I think Morley's been a friend of hers for about three years."

The three were silent, each busy with the same thought: that Morley was being blamed for a series of acts at this time which duplicated what had happened four years ago when he was unknown to the Fulton family, with this distinction, that this last time murder had been added to the blackmail or whatever it was. And the theory of his guilt was weakened.

"Mr. Withers has told me," Bristow said, "that there was a repetition of the pawning of the jewels in Washington about a year ago."

"That's true," confirmed Fulton. "But on that occasion I knew nothing of what had happened until Enid came to me, again with the request that I redeem the jewelry. Her husband had arrived in Washington unexpectedly, precipitating the crisis. I gave her the money. The sum this time was eight thousand dollars."

"And that ended it, Mr. Fulton?"

The old man looked out again toward the mountains as if he sought to gain some of their serenity.

"No. That time I asked her what troubled her. I explained that I would blame her for nothing, that I only wanted to help her, to give her comfort. But she wouldn't tell me anything. She declared that nobody could help her and that, anyway, there would never be a repetition of the extortion.

"She wept bitterly—I can hear her weeping now—and she begged me to believe that she had been guilty of nothing—nothing criminal or immoral. I told her I could never believe that of her.

"'It doesn't affect me alone. I'll have to fight

it out the best way I can,' was all the explanation she could bring herself to give me. The one fact she revealed was that the man concerned in the Atlantic City affair had also been responsible for her trouble in Washington."

Bristow, absorbed in every word of the story, recollected at once that Mrs. Allen had received the same explanation when she had tried to comfort Mrs. Withers.

"By George!" said Braceway, his voice a little husky. "She was game all right—game to the finish."

"I think," said Fulton, relaxing suddenly so that his whole form seemed to sag and grow weak, "that's all I wanted to tell you. It's all I can tell —all I know. I wanted to show you that this man with the gold tooth and the brown beard is no myth, as you seem to believe.

"Make no mistake about him, gentlemen. He has ability, ability which he uses only for unworthy ends." The old man sucked in his lips and bit on them. "He's elusive, slippery, working always in the dark.

"He's low, base. He wouldn't stop at murder. And I'm certain he was the principal figure in my daughter's death. Nothing—no power on earth—nobody can ever make me believe that Enid was murdered by the negro. It doesn't fit in with what has gone before."

"If there's any way to find this man, we'll do it," Bristow assured him.

Braceway sprang to his feet.

"You can bet your last dollar on that, Mr. Fulton," he said heartily. "If he's to be found, we'll get him."

The old man got to his feet. The recital of his story had weakened him. His legs were a little unsteady. Braceway took him by the arm, and they started down the steps.

"Will I see you again this afternoon?" Bristow called to the Atlanta detective.

"I rather think so," Braceway threw back over his shoulder. "As soon as I've had lunch I want to talk to Abrahamson. Chief Greenleaf seems to have neglected him."

Bristow hesitated a moment, then limped down the steps.

"I beg your pardon, Mr. Fulton," he said, overtaking the two, "but is there nothing more, no hint, no probable clue, you can give us about this mysterious man?"

"Absolutely nothing," Fulton answered wearily. "I've told you all I know."

"You gave him—rather, you gave your daughter for him a total of seventeen thousand dollars, counting the loan of two thousand and the cost of redeeming the jewels both times. I beg your pardon for seeming insistent, but is it possible that you passed over that much money without even asking why she had been obliged to use it? Not many people would credit such a thing."

Fulton smiled, and for a moment his grief seemed lightened by the hint of happy memories.

"Ah, you didn't know my daughter, sir," he said. "She was irresistible, not to be denied—one of the ardent flames of life. If she had asked me, I would have given her treble that amount—anything, anything, sir."

Bristow thought of what had been said of her in Atlanta: that all women liked her and that any man who had shaken hands with her was her unquestioning servant. Surely such a woman would have been irresistible in her requests to her father.

He ventured another line of inquiry:

"When you arrived at Number Five this morning, I was in the living room, and I saw the meeting between you and Miss Maria Fulton. I came away as soon as I could, but I couldn't help noting your expression as you greeted her. It seemed to me that there was accusation in it."

"There was," the old man assented. "Enid had written me that Maria had been pressing her for money, too much money. Naturally, when I heard of the—the tragedy, I coupled it with the old, old thing that had always been a burden on Enid—money. And this time I blamed Maria. Of course, however, that was a mistake."

"I see," said Bristow.

He returned to his porch and sat down. He went over all that the father of the dead woman had told him. So far as he could see, it had only served the purpose of strengthening the case against Morley. Let it be discovered that Maria had known Morley at the time of the Atlantic City affair, and the case would be fixed, irrefutable. And Braceway would win out.

Of course, there was still one chance. There was the bare possibility that Morley had gone to No. 5 to murder Enid if he did not get more money from her, and that he had been frustrated by the fact that the negro Perry had forestalled him and done the murder first. Having advanced it, Bristow did not care to abandon the theory that Perry was the guilty man.

An automobile whirled up Manniston Road and stopped in front of No. 9. His physician, Dr. Mowbray, sprang from the car and up the steps.

"Good morning, doctor!" the patient called out cheerily.

"Hello!" answered Mowbray crustily. "But what's the big idea in your trying to do a Sherlock Holmes in this murder case?"

The doctor was overbearing and opinionated. He had many patients, who were in the habit of kotowing to him and obeying his instructions implicitly. It was something which he required.

"Sit down," invited Bristow. "I'm not doing any Sherlock Holmes stuff, but I thought I ought to help out if I could."

"Well, you can't!" snapped Mowbray, with quick, nervous gestures. "You'll be in your grave before you know it. You can't stand this." He shot out his hand and produced his watch with the celerity of a sleight-of-hand performer. "Let me feel your pulse."

Bristow surrendered his wrist to the professional fingers.

"Just what I thought—twenty beats too fast. And your respiration's a crime. Have you had any rest at all, today or yesterday?"

"Not much, doctor."

Mowbray glowered at him.

"Well, you'll have to have it! You ought to be in bed this minute. If you don't carry out my instructions, I'll drop the case. You know that."

"I'm sorry, doctor, but I can't spend my time in bed now," Bristow said as persuasively as he could.

"I'd like to know why! Why? Why?"

"I'm going to Washington tomorrow, although that's a secret. I merely confide it to you in a professional way, and——"

"Going to Washington! Man, you're mad—mad! You'll have a hemorrhage or something, and die—die, I tell you!"

"Nevertheless," Bristow insisted, "I must go."

"About this murder?"

"Yes."

"Very well!" snorted Mowbray, rising like a jumping-jack. "Go—go to the North Pole if you wish. I'm through! I can't treat a man who defies my orders and advice. Good morning, sir."

Bristow gave him no answer, and he ran down the steps and threw himself into his car.

"Mistuh Bristow, Lucy's done come," said Mattie, at the living room door.

Bristow started to leave his chair, but changed his mind.

"Tell her to wait a few minutes," he said.

He began to think and to determine just what he wanted to find out from Lucy, what she would say and what he wanted her to say. It would not do to question her before he felt sure of what she knew and what she must confess. He rocked gently in his chair, going over several times the evidence he desired. His face was hard-set, almost like marble, as he stared at the mountains. He was thinking harder at that moment than he had done at any time since the murder.

He had it now. She had given Perry the key to the Withers kitchen—or, better still, Perry had taken it from her—and she remembered every detail of it, his departure from her house and his return with the key. That was what she had to confess. Inevitably, he argued, that would be her story, or else she would have no story at all.

He thought of Braceway. He made now no secret of the fact that a struggle between himself and the Atlanta man was on—not openly, but thoroughly understood by both of them—a fight for supremacy, a contest in which he sought to convict Perry while Braceway worked for the conviction of Morley.

Braceway had the added incentive of wanting to run down the man who had destroyed his friend's home life; and Braceway believed that Morley and Morley's money entanglements had, in some way, caused the tragedy.

Well, he, Bristow, would see about that! He knew he had the best of the argument so far—and he looked forward to a double pleasure: the applause that would come to him as the result of Perry's conviction, and his own personal gratification at besting Braceway at his own game.

He went into the unused bedroom and told Mattie to send Lucy Thomas to him there. While he waited, he closed the two windows.

CHAPTER XIII

LUCY THOMAS TALKS

LUCY came slowly into the room and stood near the door. She was of the peculiar-looking negress type sometimes seen in the South—light of complexion, with hard, porcelain-like blue eyes and kinky hair which, instead of being black, is brown or brownish red. After her first startled glance toward Bristow she stood with her head lowered and with an expression of sulky stubbornness.

"Sit down!" he ordered after a few moments' silence, indicating a chair near the wall.

She took her seat while he stepped to the door and closed it.

"Now, Lucy," he said, pulling at his lower lip as he stood in the middle of the room and looked down at her, "I'm not going to hurt you, and there's nothing for you to be afraid of. All I want you to do is to tell me the truth."

In spite of his reassuring words, the woman caught the full meaning of the goading sharpness in his voice. She immediately became more sullen.

"'Deed, I ain' got nothin' to tell 'bout you white folks," she said, with a touch of insolence.

"This isn't about white folks," he corrected her, resisting his quick impulse to anger. "It's about coloured folks."

"Nothin' 'bout dem neithuh," she continued in the same tone. "I don' know nothin' 'cep'n I wuz drunk. I done tole all dat down at de p'lice station."

"Listen to me!" he commanded, a little pale. "You know perfectly well what I want to find out. I want you to tell me everything you remember about Perry Carpenter's actions and words last Monday night—the night before last."

She raised and lowered her eyes rapidly, the lids working like the shutter of a camera.

"I knows what you wants, an' I knows I don' know nothin' 'tall 'bout it," she objected, her sullenness a patent defiance.

He stared at her for a full two minutes. She could hear the breath whistling between his teeth; the sound of it frightened her.

"Don't lie to me!" he said, now a trifle hoarse. "It isn't necessary, and it doesn't do anybody any good—you or Perry either."

She began to whimper.

Looking at her, he was conscious of being absorbed in the attempt to keep his temper instead of eliciting what she had to tell. He smiled.

"Stop that sniffling, and tell me what you know about Monday night! Don't you remember that Perry told you he was going to Mrs. Withers' house and steal her jewelry?"

"I done tole you I don' remembuh nothin'."

He took a step toward her and lifted his open hand as if to strike her in the face. Without waiting for the blow, she slid from the chair and fell sprawling to the floor, where she lay, moaning.

"Get up!"

She obeyed him, her arms held folded over her head as a shield against expected blows. She was still sullen, uncommunicative, her head down.

He limped swiftly to the door, left the room and went to the front part of the house. He paced the length of the living room several times, his fists clenched, his protuberant lip grown heavier.

He called to Mattie, who was in the kitchen.

"I wish," he directed, "you'd go down to Sterrett's and get a dozen oranges."

"Yes, suh. Right now, Mistuh Bristow?"

"Yes; hurry. I want some orangeade."

He returned to the bedroom and closed the door. Lucy was bent forward on the chair, moaning.

"Stop that!" he said, feeling now that he had himself and her under control. "If you don't stop, you'll have something real to sniffle about before I'm through with you! Now begin. What about Perry last Monday night?"

"Please, suh," she changed her tone, "lemme go. I ain' got nothin' to say. I feels like I might say somethin' dat ain' so. I'se kinder skeered you might make me say somethin' whut I don' mean to say."

Moving deliberately, a fine, little tremor in his fingers, he took off his coat and vest and hung them on the back of a chair. He had just noticed that it was warm and close in the shut-up room. There was a ringing in his ears. He kept repeating to himself that, if he lost his temper, she would never become communicative.

He began all over again, patient, persistent——

When Mattie came back with the oranges, she met Lucy just outside the kitchen door. There were no tears in the Thomas woman's eyes, but she seemed greatly distressed.

"Whut 'd he want offen you?" Mattie asked, with the negro's usual curiosity.

"Nothin' much," replied the other, looking blankly out across Mattie's shoulder. "He jes' axed me whut I knowd 'bout Perry dat night."

"I tole you dar warn't nothin' to be skeered uv him foh," said Mattie. "Some uv you niggers ain' got no sense."

"Yas; dat's so," Lucy agreed dully, and walked slowly away.

She moved as if she felt that there was something frightful behind her. When she was half-way home, she broke into a run, and, moaning, ran the remainder of the distance. She threw herself on her bed and sobbed a long time.

She had talked, and for the present she thought she felt more sorry for Perry than she did for herself.

In the meantime, Bristow had gone into the bathroom to wash his hands.

"Pah!" he exclaimed, disgusted.

He dried his hands and walked, whistling, out to the living room. No matter how distasteful the scene with the sullen woman had been, the substantial fact remained that he had in his pocket an important document. After all, Lucy Thomas had talked—and signed.

"Mattie," he called, "fix me an orangeade,

please. Mr. Greenleaf's late for dinner, and I need a little freshening up."

He went to the living room window again and gazed, with thoughtful, slightly sad eyes, out toward the mountains.

"These policemen!" he was thinking contemptuously. "They don't know how to make blockheads tell what they can tell. There are ways—and ways."

CHAPTER XIV

THE PAWN BROKER TAKES THE TRAIL

FRANK ABRAHAMSON, pawn broker and junk dealer, responded at once to Braceway's warm smile. The Jew had his racial respect for keenness and clean-cut ability. He liked this man who, dressed like a dandy, spoke with the air of authority.

"The fellow with the gold tooth?" he replied to Braceway's request for information. "Was there anything peculiar about him? Why, yes. He was clothed in peculiarities."

The pawn broker, thin, round-shouldered, with a great hook-nose and cavernous, bright eyes, spoke rapidly, without an accent, punctuating his sentences with thrusts and dartings and waves of his two hands. His fifty-five years had not lessened his vitality.

"You see, Mr. Braceway, we pawn brokers, we have to observe our customers. We become judges of human nature. At the best, we have a hard time making a living." Somehow, with his smile, he discounted this statement. "And we come to judge men as closely as we examine jewels and precious metals. You see?"

Braceway saw. He lit a cigarette and stepped to the door to throw away the match. The Jew appreciated the thoughtfulness. Trash on the floor made the morning task of sweeping up harder.

"Now," continued Abrahamson, expressing with one movement of his arm tolerant ridicule, "this man with the gold tooth and the brown beard—he thought he was disguised. By gracious! it was funny. A fellow like me takes one look at him and sees the disguise. The gold tooth—that was false, fake. When he talked to me, it was all I could do to keep from reaching across the counter and pushing that tooth more firmly into his jaw. Gold is heavy, you see. I was afraid it might drop down on my showcase and break some glass."

Abrahamson laughed. So did Braceway.

"And his beard, Mr. Braceway? That was better. To the ordinary observer, it might have looked natural—but not to me. Oh, yes; he was disguised—too much.—Besides, the other afternoon was not the first time I had seen him—no."

"You saw him two months ago, then?"

"Yes, sir—two months ago, and one month before that."

"In here?"

"Yes."

"What did he want?"

"Money. Money for jewelry. Oh, he had the jewelry. And I gave him the money—a great deal; more, perhaps, than was good for me, when you remember I always try to make a reasonable profit. He argued. He knew about values."

This interested Braceway more than anything he had yet heard.

"That gave you an idea," he suggested.

"You are quick, Mr. Braceway. It did give me an idea. It made me think: well! This man, he has pawned things before, these very same things. He knew quite well what they should bring." Abrahamson shrugged his shoulders. "And he did know—and I let him have the money. That is, I mean, what happened the first two times. This last time, the three days ago, he was different, in a hurry, and he took only what I offered. He made no argument. I could see he was frightened. Yes—he was different this last time."

The detective, oblivious of the other for a moment, blew a cloud of smoke across the counter, causing the Jew to dodge and cough.

"Let me see," Braceway said. "You saw him three months ago, two months ago, and three days ago. Had you ever seen him before?"

Abrahamson laughed, and, reaching over, slapped Braceway on the shoulder gently.

"You are so quick, Mr. Braceway! I can't swear I had ever seen him before, but I think I had—not with the gold tooth and the beard, but with a moustache and bushy eyebrows, eyebrows too bushy."

"Where? Where did you see him?"

"Here, I think—but I'm not sure, you see. Sometimes I have traveled a little—to Atlanta, to Washington, to New York. I don't know; I can't tell whether I saw him in one of those places, or some other place, or here."

Braceway urged him with his eyes.

"If you only could! Mr. Abrahamson, if you could remember where you saw him when he wore the moustache, you would enable me to put my hands on him. You'd do more. You'd give me enough information to lead to the arrest of the murderer."

Abrahamson was silent, gazing through the shop doorway. He turned to the detective again.

"I bet you, Mr. Braceway, you will be glad to hear something. Chief Greenleaf was in here this morning, asking questions. But he asked so many that were worth nothing, so few that were good. And I forgot to tell him the whole story—the things of, perhaps, significance."

"Tell me. Significance is what I'm after."

"Well, you know Mr. Withers spent almost the whole day in here before the night of the murder. Once he went out. That was in the late afternoon to get some lunch. While he was out—understand, while he was out—in came the gold-tooth fellow.

"It was bad luck. I kept him as long as I could, but he was hurried, nervous. Half an hour, forty minutes maybe, after the gold-tooth fellow had gone, in came Withers again, out of breath, complaining that he had picked the man up just outside here and followed him, only to lose him when the gold-tooth fellow went through Casey's store to the avenue.

"I showed Withers the ring the fellow had pawned for a hundred dollars.

"'Yes, yes!' he said; 'that's one of my wife's rings.'

"And he was all cut up.

"Now, here is what I have to tell." Abrahamson lowered his voice and, leaning low on his elbow, thrust his face far over the counter toward Braceway. "It is only an idea, but—it is an idea. I bet you I would not tell anybody else. Such things might get a man into trouble. But I like you, Mr. Braceway. I confide in you. Mr. Withers and that man with the beard and the gold tooth—something in the look of the eyes, something in the build of the shoulders—each reminded me of the other, a little. And they were at no time in here together. Just an idea, I told you. But——"

He spread out his hands, straightened his back, and smiled.

Braceway was, undisguisedly, amazed.

"You mean Withers was the——"

"S—sh—sh!" Abrahamson held up a protesting hand. "Not so loud, Mr. Braceway. It is just an idea for you to think over. I study faces, and all that sort of thing, and ideas sometimes are valuable—sometimes not."

"By George!" Braceway put into his expression an enthusiasm he was far from feeling. "You've done me a service, a tremendous service, Mr. Abrahamson."

He thought rapidly. Three months ago! Where had George Withers been then? Three months ago was the first of February. He started. It was then that Withers had gone to Savannah. At least, he had said he was going to Savannah. And two months ago? He was not certain, but when had George left Atlanta, ostensibly for Memphis?

Inwardly, the detective ridiculed himself. He would have sworn to the innocence of Withers. In fact, he was swearing to it all over again as he stood there in the pawnshop. Abrahamson's "idea" was out of the question. People were often victims of "wild thinking" in the midst of the excitement caused by a murder mystery.

He returned to the effort to persuade the Jew to try to remember where he had seen the bearded man without a beard, with only a moustache and bushy eyebrows.

"That's the important thing," he urged. "If you can remember that, I'll land the murderer."

"Maybe—perhaps, I can." The pawn broker hesitated, then made up his mind to confide to Braceway another secret. "I don't promise, but there is a chance. You see, Mr. Braceway, I'm a thinker." He smiled, deprecating the statement. "Most men do not think. But me, I think. I do this: I want to remember something. Good! I go back into my little room back of the shop, and I practise association of ideas. What does the moustache remind me of? What was in his voice that made me think I had seen him before? What do his eyes bring up in my mind?

"So! I go back over the months, over the years. One idea leads to another connected with it. There flash into my mind links and links of thoughts until I have a chain leading to—where? Somewhere. It is fun—and it brings the results. I will do so tonight and tomorrow. I will try. I bet you I will be able to tell you—finally. You see?"

"It's a great scheme," said Braceway, encouraging him. "It ought to work. Now, tell me this: how did this fellow strike you? What did you think of him when he was in here pawning jewels and wearing a disguise?"

"I will tell you the truth. I thought at first he was like a lot of other sick people who come here with that disease—tuberculosis. In the beginning they have plenty of money. They expect to get well before the money gives out. But they have miscalculated. They are not yet well, and the money is gone.

"What next? They must have more money. With this disease, the rich get well, the poor die. Well! I thought this fellow needed money to get well—that was all; and, like a lot of them, he was ashamed of being hard up and didn't want it known."

"Tell me this: would the ordinary man in the street have noticed that the gold tooth was a false, clumsy affair?"

"I think not. I buy all sorts of old gold and sets of false teeth. There is a market for them. I have studied them. That's why I saw what this fellow's was."

"I see. Now, will you show me what he pawned two months ago, and three months ago?"

Abrahamson consulted a big book, went to the safe at the back of the shop, and returned with two little packets. In the first were two bracelets, one studded with emeralds and diamonds, the other set with rubies. In the second envelope was a gold ring set with one large diamond surrounded by small rubies.

"I allowed him six hundred dollars on the bracelets," explained Abrahamson; "they are handsome—exquisite; and three hundred and fifty on the ring."

Braceway passed the stuff back to him. It was a part of the Withers jewelry.

"You see, Mr. Braceway," added the Jew, "all this business, this murder and everything, will cost me money. This jewelry, it is stolen goods. Chief Greenleaf leaves it here for the present, as a decoy. Perhaps, somebody might try to reclaim it. That's what he thinks. As for me, I don't think so. It is a dead loss."

He sighed and rearranged the articles in their envelopes.

"Yes," agreed the detective; "it's hard luck. You've got every reason to be interested in running down the truth in this mix-up. I wish you could tell me where you think you saw this man—the time he had neither the gold tooth nor the brown beard."

"Be patient, my friend—Mr. Braceway. By tomorrow I may remember. I shall work hard—the association of ideas! It is a great system."

Braceway thanked him and was about to leave the shop. He had already formed a new plan. He turned back to the pawn broker.

"By the way," he said, "I'm going to Washington tomorrow. If you should remember, if the association of ideas produces anything, I wonder if you'd wire me?"

"Certainly. Certainly."

The detective wrote on a slip of paper: S. S. Braceway, Willard Hotel. He handed it to Abrahamson.

"Wire me that address, collect," he directed.

Abrahamson promised, smiling. He was pleased with the idea of helping to solve the problem which convulsed Furmville.

"Oh," added Braceway, "another thing. How would you describe this fellow in addition to the fact that he wore the beard and the gold tooth?"

"Very thin lips," replied Abrahamson slowly, "and high, straight, aquiline nose, and blond hair, and—and, I should say, rather thin, high voice."

"Good!" Braceway exclaimed. "Good! Mr. Abrahamson, you've just described the man who, I believe, committed the murder. And I know where he is."

Morley had been pointed out to him in the hotel earlier in the day, and Abrahamson's memory sketched a fairly good likeness of the young man as he remembered him. Why not make certain of it at once?

"You've been very obliging," he continued, "and, I suppose, that's why I feel I can impose on you further. I confide in you, as you did in me. I'm going back to the Brevord now. Could you follow me and take a look at a man who'll be with me there?"

The Jew's eyes sparkled.

"Yes, Mr. Braceway," he said and added: "It may cost me money, closing up the shop, you understand. But if I can help——"

"Don't misunderstand me," the detective cautioned. "There's no charge of murder. Nothing like that. This fellow may be the gold-tooth man, and still not be the guilty man."

"I see; I see," Abrahamson's tone was one of importance. "You go on, Mr. Braceway. I'll follow in three minutes."

"If the man I'm with is the one who wore the disguise, if he looks more like it than Mr. Withers did, make no sign. If he's not the fellow communicate with me later—as soon as you can."

Morley was the first person Braceway saw when he entered the lobby of the hotel. He lost no time, but crossed over to the leather settee on which the young man sat. Morley looked haggard and frightened, and, although he held a newspaper in front of him, was gazing into space.

Braceway decided to "take a chance." He had a great respect for his intuitions. These "hunches," he had found, were sometimes of no value, but they had helped him often enough to make the ideas that came to him in this way worth trying. He introduced himself.

"I was wondering," he said, sitting down beside Morley, "if you couldn't help me out in a little matter."

Morley sighed and put down his paper before he answered:

"What is it?"

"Something about make-ups—facial make-up."

Morley looked at him and felt that the detective's eyes bored into him.

"What about make-up?"

"I had the idea—perhaps I got it from George Withers—that you used to be interested in a matter of theatricals."

Morley coloured.

"Yes. That is," he qualified, "I was a member of the dramatic club when I was in college, University of Pennsylvania. But I didn't know Withers knew anything about it."

Braceway's demeanour now was casual. His eyes were no longer on Morley. He was watching Abrahamson, who was at the news-stand near the main entrance.

"I thought George had mentioned it to me, but I may be mistaken. Did you ever 'make up' with a beard?"

The morning papers had got hold of the suspicion of some of the authorities that a man wearing a brown beard and a gold tooth was wanted because of the murder of Mrs. Withers. Although Chief Greenleaf had tried to keep it quiet, it had leaked out as a result of Jenkins' search for traces of the man. Morley had read all this, and Braceway's question upset him.

"No," he answered; "I never did. I played women's parts."

Abrahamson was shaking his head in negation. He made it plain that he saw in Morley no resemblance to the man who had come disguised to the pawnshop.

Braceway did not press Morley for further information.

"Then you can't help me," he laughed lightly. "Women don't wear beards."

He got up with a careless word about the hot weather and passed on to the clerk's desk. He was thinking: "He was lying. Any college annual prints the cast of the important 'show' given by the dramatic club that year. I'll wire Philadelphia."

He found the manager of the Brevord and inquired:

"How about the bellboy who was on duty all Monday night, Mr. Keene?"

"He's in the house now," Keene informed him. "Roddy is his name."

"Send him up to my room, will you?"

Braceway stepped into the elevator. Five minutes after he had disappeared, Morley went into the writing room. His hand trembled a little as he picked up a pen. He put two or three lines on several sheets of paper, one after the other, and tore up all of them.

The communication which he finally completed he put into an envelope and addressed to Braceway. It read:

"Dear Mr. Braceway: When you asked me about the make-up, I was thinking of something else and was not quite clear as to what you were saying or what you wanted to know. I remember now that, on one occasion, I did have a part as a man who wore a beard in a play given by my college dramatic club. However, I don't remember enough about it to pass as an expert on such make-ups.

"Yours truly,

"Henry Morley."

Going to the desk, he left the note for the detective.

"I'm a fool," he reflected, as he went to the door and looked out at the traffic in the street. "I believe I'll get a lawyer."

He considered this for a while.

"Oh, what's the use? He'll ask me a lot of questions, and——"

He shuddered and turned back into the lobby, hesitant and wretched.

"My God!" he thought miserably. "I've got to get back to Washington! I've got to! After that, I can think—think!"

But he believed he could not go until the chief of police gave him permission. If he had consulted a lawyer, he might have found out differently. As it was, he stayed on, thinking more and more disconnectedly, eating nothing, his nerves wearing to raw ends.

Upstairs Braceway was strengthening the net he had already woven around Henry Morley.

"I was right." He reviewed what he had learned from Abrahamson. "It's still up to Morley. That pawn broker's off, 'way off. He thinks George Withers resembles the man with the beard, and, although he gave me the description that fitted Morley exactly, he takes a look at him and denies emphatically that Morley resembles at all the fellow with the disguise."

Abrahamson, however, was not satisfied with what he had seen. Back in front of his shop, he opened the door, took down the sign he had left hanging on the knob, "Back in ten minutes," substituted another, "Closed for the day," relocked the door, and started off in the direction of Casey's department store.

He had decided to devote the whole afternoon to detective work. Of course, it would cost him money, having the shop closed half a day. "But," he consoled himself, "I'm worth seventy thousand dollars. I bet I am entitled to a little holiday."

CHAPTER XV

BRACEWAY SEES A LIGHT

BRACEWAY had discovered long ago that the man who attempts good work as a detective must depend almost as much on his ability to make friends as he does on his capacity for sifting evidence.

"I'm a good worker," he was in the habit of saying, "but I'm not half as good working alone as I am when I have the help of all the men and women who are witnesses in a case or connected with it in some other way. I need all the coöperation I can get."

This was one reason why Roddy, when he entered Braceway's room, felt sure immediately that he would receive only kindly treatment. He had shown signs of fear on entering the room, and in his extremely black face his singularly white eyeballs had rolled around grotesquely.

But Braceway put him at ease with a smile.

"What have you been trying to do, Roddy?" was his first good-humoured question. "Think you've got sense enough to fool all the white folks?"

"Who, boss? Me, boss?" the boy returned, disavowing with a grin any pretense to intelligence. "Naw, suh, boss. You knows I ain' got no sense. I ain' nevuh tried to fool nobody."

"Didn't you tell the chief of police you were awake all of Monday night when you were on duty in the lobby and didn't you say the only thing you did was to carry up Mr. Morley's bags?"

"Yas, suh, boss; an' dat was de truth—nothin' but de truth, boss. Gawd knows——"

Braceway took from his pocket a crisp, new one-dollar bill and smoothed it out on his knee.

"Now, listen to me, Roddy," he said, this time unsmiling. "Mr. Keene has just told me he wouldn't fire you, even if you did go to sleep Monday night. There's nothing for you to be afraid of; and this dollar note is yours as soon as you tell me the truth, the real truth, about what you saw and what you missed seeing Monday night. If you don't tell me, I'll have you arrested."

Roddy's eyes, which had shone with a rather greasy glitter at the sight of the money, rolled rapidly and whitely in their sockets at the mention of arrest.

"'Deed, boss, you ain' gwine to have no cause to 'res' me, no cause whatsomever. You knows how 'tis, boss. Us coloured folks, we got a gif', jes' a natchel gif', foh nappin' an' sleepin'. Boss, dar ain' no nigger in dis town whut would have kep' wide awake—*wide*—all dat Monday night nor any yuther night."

"Very well. Think now. Try to remember. Were you asleep at all before midnight?"

"Naw, suh, boss. Naw, suh!"

"Not at all?"

Roddy began to wilt again.

"Well, it might uv been dis way, boss, possibilly. 'Long 'bout 'leven I kinder remembuhs jes' a sort uv nap, mo' like a slip, boss." He coughed and spoke desperately: "You see, boss, when it gits a little quiet at night, seems to me, why, right den, ev'y nigger I knows is got a hinge in his neck. 'Pears like he jes' gotter let his haid drap furward. Dar ain' no use talkin', boss, dat hinge wuks ovuh-time. I 'spec' mine done it, too, jes' like you say, 'long 'bout 'leven. Yas, suh, I reckon dat's right."

"How about the time between midnight and two in the morning? Was the hinge working then?"

"Aw, boss," replied Roddy with something like reproach, "you knows 'tain' no queshun uv a hinge arftuh midnight. Arftuh midnight, boss, de screws drap right outen' de hinge, an' dar ain' no mo' hinge. You jes' natchelly keeps your haid down an' don' lif' it no mo'. Naw, suh, dar ain' no hinge to he'p you dat late, *on*less—*on*less somebody hit you or stab you."

Braceway became stern. His eyes snapped.

"Didn't you carry Mr. Morley's grips up to his room for him that night, room number four hundred and twenty-one?"

"Yas, suh."

"What time was that?"

"Dat wuz jes' five minutes arftuh two, boss."

"Had you been asleep during the two hours before that?"

"I hates to say it, boss, but I wuz, almos' completely."

"Then, how did you wake yourself up thoroughly enough to know that it was exactly five minutes past two?"

"Lemme see, suh. Possibilly, 'twuz bekase uv whut I seen 'long about ha'fpas' one—possibilly, boss."

"So you hadn't been asleep for two hours?"

"Almos', suh. It wuz dis way: you see, boss, de bellboys' bench is right unduh de big clock in de lobby, off to de right uv de desk. I happen' dat night to let my haid slide ovuh 'g'in de glass case uv de clock, an when it stahted out to hit de ha'f-pas' bell, it rattled an' whizzed, an' it jarred me. Golly, boss! I woke up an', when I seed how it wuz rainin' outside, I thought lightnin' had hit me. It skeered me—an' dat is one good way to wake up a nigger at night—skeer 'im, an' you don' have to stab him. I sorter hollered.

"I got up an' went to de main entrance, jes' to make de night clerk think I wuz on de job in case he woke up. I looked down de street tow'rd de post-office, an' I seed a man goin' in dar.

"'Bless de Lawd!' I says to myse'f. 'White people ain' got much to do—goin' to de post-office dis time uv night.' An' I went on back to de bell-boys' bench and stahted in niggerin' it once mo'e."

"Niggering it?"

"Yas, boss; you know, dat means quick sleepin'. 'Peared to me I ain' no mo'e got my eyes shut when I wakes up ag'in, an' right dar in de lobby is dat same man what I seed gwine to de post-office."

"What waked you up?"

"I don' know, boss. I can' no mo'e figger dat out den I kin fly. Dat wuz de fust time in my life dat I done wake up at night when *on*molested."

"How did you know the man you saw in the

lobby was the one you had seen going into the post-office?"

"Dey wuz de same, boss; dat's all. Had de same buil', same long raincoat on, an' same thick beard. He had done pass' me by an' wuz on his way up de stairs 'stead uv waitin' foh me to run de elevatuh. I wouldn' nevuh seed his beard dat time, but he turn' 'roun' when he wuz nigh to de top uv de stairs an' look back at me. Den I seed foh a fac' dat he wuz de same as de yuther man I jes' done seed."

Braceway gave no sign of how highly he valued the negro's words. Seated by the window, the dollar bill still on his knee, he kept his gaze on Roddy, holding him to his narrative.

"You want me to believe that, when you saw this man two blocks away at half-past one in the morning, you noticed he wore a beard? Wasn't it too dark?"

"Naw, suh. Dem post-office lights is pow'ful, boss. I seed de beard all right, an' I seed it once mo'e when he wuz on de stairs."

"What did he do after he had looked back at you while he was going upstairs?"

"Nothin', boss. He seed I wuz lookin' at him, an' he jes' went on up an' out uv sight, in a hurry, like."

"What time was that?"

"Dat wuz twenty-six minutes uv two."

"How do you know that? You'd gone back to sleep, hadn't you?"

"Yas, suh, a little niggerin'. But, when I woke up dat way widout no reason, I kinder jumped. I wuz afeer'd dat clock might be goin' to jar me ag'in, an' I took a look at it. Dat wuz how I seed de time. It wuz twenty-six minutes uv two."

"What did you do then?"

"Nothin', boss; jes' went on niggerin' it. Dat is, I went on till de night clerk giv' me a kick on de shins an' tole me to take Mistuh Morley's bags up to fo'-twenty-one. I done tole you dat was five minutes arftuh two. Den, when we got up to de room, I says to him: 'I thought you wuz in dis hotel half-hour ago, boss, when you had a beard.'

"An' right off de bat I wuz sorry I said dat. He look' at me kinder mad an' he said: 'Whut you talkin' 'bout, boy? You mus' be talkin' in yore sleep!'

"I come on back downstairs. He didn' have to say no mo'e. I tell you, boss, when a white man tell me I been talkin' in my sleep, I *is* been talkin' in my sleep—dar ain' no argufyin' 'bout it—I *is* been doin' dat ve'y thing."

"But you thought Mr. Morley, the man with the grips, was the one you had seen going up the stairs and, also, the one you had seen going into the post-office—and, when you saw him on the stairs and on the street, he wore a beard? Is that it?"

"I ain' thought nothin' 'bout it, boss. I knowed it."

"What did you think about his shaving off the beard at that time in the morning?" Braceway urged, fingering the dollar bill. "Didn't you think it was queer?"

" I tryin' to tell you, suh, I ain' done no thinkin' 'bout dat. He done said I wuz talkin' in my sleep, an' I is a prudent nigger."

" Did he have a gold tooth, Roddy? "

" Naw, suh," said Roddy, " but he did look rich 'nough to have one. Leastways I ain' seen he had one."

" Have you seen the man with the beard since? "

" Naw, suh. I jes' tole you, boss, he done shave it off."

" And Mr. Morley? "

" Yas, suh, I done seen him. He's in de hotel now. He's de same man."

" Did he wear rubber overshoes when he had the beard, and when he didn't have it? "

" Yas, suh—bofe times."

" Has he said anything to you since Monday night? "

" Naw, suh."

" Did you see anybody else that night—Monday night? "

" Naw, suh."

" Do you remember anything else about how the bearded man looked? "

" Naw, suh, 'cep' he look' jes' like dis Mistuh Morley; dat's all I know, boss."

Braceway got to his feet.

" All right, Roddy," he said heartily; " you're a good boy. Here's your dollar."

Roddy rolled his white eyeballs toward the ceiling and bent his black face floorward.

" Gawd bless you, boss! You is one good——"

" And here's another dollar, if you can keep your

mouth shut about this until I tell you to open it. Can you do that?"

Roddy conveyed the assurance of his ability to remain dumb until a considerable time after the sounding of Gabriel's trump.

"See that you do. If you don't, I might have to arrest you after all."

When the negro had gone, Braceway stood at the window and, with glance turned toward the street, saw nothing of what was passing there. He was reviewing the facts—or possible facts—that had just come to him. Restlessness took hold of him. He fell to pacing the length of the room with long, quick strides. It seemed that, in the labour of forcing his brain to its highest activity, he called on every fibre and muscle of his physique. His cheeks were flushed; his eyes, hard and brilliant, snapped.

He was thinking—thinking, going over every particle of the evidence he had drawn from Roddy, trying to estimate its value when compared with everything else he had learned about the case. His stride grew more rapid; his breathing was faster.

The murder, the men and women connected with it, the stories they had told, all these flashed on the screen of his mind and hung there until he had judged them to their smallest detail.

What could Abrahamson have meant by indicating a belief that the man with the gold tooth looked like George Withers?

Was the boy Roddy wide enough awake that night to have formed any real opinion as to the resemblance of the bearded man and Henry Morley?

The trip to the post-office—did that explain the disappearance of the stolen jewelry? Had Morley mailed it at once to himself, or somebody else, in Washington?

Withers had returned to the Brevord early Monday night. That must have been before half-past twelve. Although the night clerk and the bellboy had been asleep at the time and had not seen him, there was no room for doubt of his return as he had described it.

And why should Morley, wearing the disguise, have waked up Roddy and assured himself, by the look flung over his shoulder, that the negro saw him on the stairs?

Or had that been Morley, after all? What reason, what motive——

Suddenly, with the abruptness of a horse thrown back on his haunches, he stood stock still in the middle of the room, his brilliant eyes staring at the wall, his breathing faster than ever, as he considered the idea that had flashed upon him. The idea grew into a theory. It had never occurred to him before, and yet it was right. It must be. He had it! For the first time, he felt sure of himself, was convinced that he held a safe grasp on the case.

He strode to the window and struck the sill with his fist. The tenseness went out of his body. He breathed a long sigh of relief. He had seen through the mist of puzzling facts and contradictory clues. The rest would be comparatively plain sailing.

Some of Braceway's friends were in the habit of laughing at him because, when he was sure of having solved a criminal puzzle, he always could be seen carrying a cane. The appearance of the cane invariably foretold the arrest of a guilty man.

He went now to the corner near the bureau and picked up the light walking-stick he had brought to Furmville strapped to his suitcase. He lingered, twirling the cane in his right hand. His thoughts went to the interview he and Bristow had had that morning with Fulton, whose white hair and deep-lined face were very clear before him. He recalled the old man's words:

"She wept bitterly. I can hear her weeping now. She had a dash, a spirit, a joyous soul. This man none of you has been able to find has been in Enid's life for a good many years."

Braceway's eyes softened.

Well, there was no need to worry now. Things were coming his way. The old man would have his revenge. He put on his hat, deciding to go down for a late lunch. When he looked at his watch, he whistled. He had promised to be at the railroad station to see the funeral party off for Atlanta on the four o'clock train; and it was now half-past three. He hurried out.

For the first time in his life, he had been guilty of taking a course which might lead to serious results, or to no results at all. He had permitted personal considerations to make "blind spots" in his brain.

Because of a warm friendship for George Withers, he had rushed to conclusions which took no account of the dead woman's husband. He had forgotten that the faces of Morley and Withers were shaped on similar lines. If any other detective had done that, Braceway would have been the first to censure him.

As he had expected, he found Withers and Mr. Fulton far ahead of train time. They had been passed through the gates and were standing on the platform. Braceway noticed that, of the two, the father was standing the ordeal with greater fortitude and calmness. Withers was nervous, fidgety, and seemed to find it impossible to stand in any one place. He drew Braceway to one side.

"I've got something to tell you, Brace," he said in a low tone, his voice tremulous. "I didn't want to tell you for—for her sake. I thought it might cause useless talk, scandal. But you're working your head off for me, and you've a right to know about it."

"Don't worry, George," Braceway reassured him. "Things are coming out all right. Don't talk if you don't feel like it."

He said this because he was suddenly aware of the quality of suffering he saw in the man's eyes. It was so evident, so striking, that he felt surprised. Perhaps, he thought, he might have exaggerated things when he had told Bristow that Enid had subjected her husband to incessant disappointments and regrets. Withers now was mourning; in fact, he appeared overwhelmed, crushed.

"It's this," Withers hurried on: "I was up there that night in front of the house until—until after one o'clock. You know I told you I was on the porch just across the road and went back to the hotel as soon as Campbell had turned his machine and gone home. That wasn't quite correct. I waited, because Enid didn't turn out the lights in the living room. It struck me as strange.

"I waited, and I fell asleep. That seems funny—a husband infuriated with his wife and trying to find out what she is doing to deceive him goes to sleep while he's watching! But that's exactly what I did.

"When I awoke, the lights were still on in the living room. I looked at my watch, and, although I couldn't see very well, I made out it was after one. I suppose I'd been asleep for half an hour at least. You see, I had had a hard night on the sleeper and a terrific day, and——"

"Sure. I understand that," Braceway consoled him. "Did you see anything, George?"

"Yes; I saw something all right," he struggled with the words. "As I looked up, a figure was silhouetted against the yellow window shade. It was a man's figure. It was after one in the morning, and a man was there with——"

His voice failed him altogether. Braceway, a perplexed look in his eyes, studied him uneasily.

"The silhouette was quite plain. There was the clear-cut shadow of him from the waist up.

It was so plain that I could see he was wearing a cap. I could see the visor of it, you know; a long visor. He was a well-built man, good shoulders, and so on.

"As I got to my feet, the lights were turned off. I went across the street. I don't think I ran. It was raining. I was going to kill him. That was all I was thinking about. I was going to kill him, and I wanted to catch him unawares. I wasn't armed, and I was going to choke him to death."

The train gates were opened, and passengers began to stream past them toward the train. Withers lowered his voice to a hoarse whisper. Braceway noticed the unpleasant sound of it.

"He did what I expected; came down the steps without a sound. I didn't even hear him close the door. I can't say I saw him. It was pitch dark, and I sensed where he was. I was conscious of all his movements. When he reached the bottom step, I closed with him. I couldn't trust to hitting at him. It was too dark.

"I put out my hands to get his throat, but I misjudged things. I caught him by the waist. He had on a raincoat. I could tell it by the feel of the cloth. And I couldn't get a good hold of him. While I struggled with him, he got me by the throat. He was a powerful man, a dozen times stronger than I am.

"We swayed around there for a few minutes, a few seconds—I don't know which. We didn't make any noise. I couldn't do a thing. He choked me until I thought my head would burst open.

"When he realized I was all in, he gave me a shove that made me reel down the walk a dozen steps. He didn't stop to see what I did. He ran. That is, I suppose he ran. I didn't hear him, and I didn't see him again. He disappeared —completely."

Braceway looked at his watch. It was five minutes before train time.

"What did you do then?"

"Nothing."

"Where did you go, then? What did you think? Speed up, George! I want to get all this before you go."

"Yes," said Withers, a little catch in his throat; "I thought you ought to know about it. I—I stood there a moment, there in the rain, dazed, trying to get my breath. I'd intended going in to have it out with Enid. But I didn't. I suppose I knew, if I did, I'd kill her. And I guess now I would have.

"You see, I hadn't the faintest notion that anything had happened to her; had hurt her, I mean. I got myself in hand. I didn't do anything. I went back to the hotel. I planned to have a last talk with her later in the day."

"Tell me," Braceway asked with undisguised eagerness, "did this man wear a beard?"

"I think so. I've been thinking about that all day. I think he did, but I'm not sure."

"But you saw the plain silhouette, the outline of his head and body!"

"Yes. He might have had a beard, and again he might not. He was heavily built, with a short, thick neck, and, in the attitude he was in, foreshortened by the light being above him, a strong chin might have been magnified, might have cast a shadow like that of a beard."

"And when you were struggling with him? How about that? Didn't you get close to his face?"

"Yes; but he was taller than I was—I don't know—I can't remember. But I think he had the beard, all right."

"He didn't make any noise on the steps, you say. Did he have rubber shoes?"

"I don't know. My guess would be that he did."

The conductor began to shout, "All aboard!"

They started toward the Atlanta pullman.

"I wouldn't have told you—I can't see that any of this could affect the final result—but for the fact that something might have come up to embarrass you," Withers explained, still with the unpleasant, rattling whisper. "It might have led you to think I hadn't been frank with you."

He had his foot on the first step of the car. The porter was evidently anxious to get aboard and close the vestibule door.

"What do you mean?" Braceway caught him by the sleeve.

"Somehow," Withers leaned down to whisper, "in the struggle, I think, I dropped—I lost my watch. Somebody must have picked it up, you know."

"Damn!" exploded Braceway angrily. "Why didn't——"

The train began to move. The porter put his hand to Withers' elbow and hurried him up the steps.

CHAPTER XVI

A MESSAGE FROM MISS FULTON

IT was a little after three o'clock when Chief Greenleaf and Lawrence Bristow finished their "celebration dinner" and took their seats on the porch of No. 9. The host, accomplishing the impossible in a prohibition state, had produced a bottle of champagne, explaining: "Just for you, chief; I never touch it; and the chief had enjoyed it, unmistakably.

At Bristow's suggestion they refrained from discussing any phase of the murder during the meal.

"All we have to do now," he said, "is to see that the knot in Perry's rope is artistically tied—and that's not appetizing."

"I've got something new," Greenleaf contributed; "but you're right. We'll wait until after dinner."

They were greatly pleased with what they had accomplished; and each one, without giving it voice, knew the other's pleasure was increased by the thought that they had got the better of Braceway.

They saw from the porch that an automobile was standing in front of No. 5. As they settled back in their chairs, Fulton and George Withers left the bungalow and got into the machine.

"They're going to take the body to Atlanta on the four o'clock," said Greenleaf.

For a moment they watched the receding automobile. Then Bristow inquired, "What's the new thing you've dug up?"

"The report from the Charlotte laboratories."

"Oh, you got that—by wire?"

The lame man seemed indifferent about it.

"Yes; by wire," Greenleaf paused, as if he enjoyed whetting the other's curiosity.

Bristow made no comment. He gave the impression of being confident that the report could contain nothing of value.

"You ain't very anxious to know what it is," the chief complained. "I nearly had a fit until it came."

"Oh, it doesn't matter much, one way or the other," Bristow said, conscious of Greenleaf's petulance. "The thing's settled anyway."

"That may be true; but it don't do any harm to get everything we can. The laboratory reported what you thought they'd report. Nothing under Miss Fulton's nails; particles of a white person's skin, epidermis, under Perry's."

Bristow laughed pleasantly, his eyes suddenly more alight.

"I beg your pardon, chief; I was having a little fun with you—by pretending indifference. But it's great—better than I'd really dared expect. It's the only direct, first-hand evidence we can offer showing that the negro, beyond any dispute, did attack her."

He laughed again. "Let's see the wire."

"I guess it settles the whole business," Greenleaf exulted, passing him the telegram.

He read it and handed it back.

"After that," he commented, "I'm almost tempted to throw away what I had to show you; its importance dwindles."

"What is it?"

"A confession by Lucy Thomas that Perry went to Number Five the night, rather the morning, of the murder."

"You got that—from her!" exclaimed Greenleaf.

"Yes—signed."

"Mr. Bristow, you're a wonder! By cripes, you are! My men couldn't get anything out of her. Neither could I."

"Here it is. I wrote out her story and read it back to her, and she signed it."

Greenleaf took the paper and read it:

"I know Perry Carpenter went to Mrs. Withers' house Monday night. He and I had been drinking together, and I was nearly drunk, but he was only about half-drunk. He told me he knew where he could get a lot of money, or 'something just as good as money,' because he had seen 'that white woman' with it. He and I had a fight because he wanted me to give him the key to Mrs. Withers' house, to her kitchen door.

"He broke the ribbon on which I used to hang the key around my neck, and he went out. That was pretty late in the night. Before daylight, he came back and flung the key on the floor, and he cursed me and hit me. I had two keys on the ribbon, one to Number Five, Manniston Road, and one to the house where I worked before I went to Mrs. Withers. He had taken the wrong one. When he hit me, he said: 'You think you're damn smart, giving me the wrong key; but that didn't stop me.' He seemed to be drunker then than he was when he went out earlier in the night.

(Signed) "Lucy Thomas."

The chief whistled. "How in thunder did you get this out of the woman?"

"Sent for her and had a talk with her. She told so many stories and contradicted herself so much that, at last, she broke down and let me have the real facts."

"Will she stick to what she says in this paper?"

"Oh, yes. There won't be any trouble about that."

Greenleaf offered him the signed confession.

"No; keep it," he said. "It's your property, not mine."

The chief folded it and put it carefully into his breast pocket.

"I wonder," he speculated, "what Mr. Braceway will say to this."

"He'll realize that the case is settled. But I don't think he'll quit work."

"Why won't he, if he sees we've got the guilty man?"

"That's what I'd like to know. I believe—this is between you and me—I believe he's working more for George Withers now than he is for the state. You see, as I've already told you, there may be some family scandal in this, something the husband wants to keep quiet. Braceway will be satisfied as soon as we show him that the only thing we want is to present the evidence against the negro; that we take no interest in private scandals. But there's one thing, however, chief, I wish you'd do: let Morley go to Washington on the midnight train tonight instead of making him wait until tomorrow."

"Why?"

"If Braceway won't let matters drop as they are now, he'll insist on following Morley to Washington. If he does, I'm going, too; and we might as well get it over."

"You're not afraid our case won't hold water, are you?"

"No. The case stands on its own feet. There's no power on earth that could break it down."

"Well, then, why——"

"I'll tell you why, chief. I've been set down here with this tuberculosis. You know what that means, at least, several years of convalescence. Why shouldn't I make use of those years, develop a business in which I can engage while I'm here? This murder case has opened the door for me, and I'm going to take advantage of it. Lawrence Bristow, consulting detective and criminologist. How does that strike you?"

"Fine!" said Greenleaf heartily. "And you're right. Your reputation's made; and, even if you had to be away from Furmville a few days at a time now and then, it wouldn't hurt your health."

The chief's tendency to claim credit for Carpenter's arrest had disappeared. He liked Bristow, was impressed by his quiet effectiveness.

"I'm glad you think I can get away with it," the lame man said, much pleased. "Now, you see why I want to go to Washington with Braceway. It's merely to keep my hold on this case. If you say I'm entitled to the credit for reading the riddle, I'm going to see that I get the credit."

"All right. I'll let Morley know he can go tonight, and he needn't worry about our troubling him."

"Thanks. The sooner we gather up every little strand of evidence, the better it will be."

Greenleaf prepared to leave. As he stood up, he caught sight of a young man coming up Manniston Road.

"A stranger," he announced. "Another detective?"

Bristow glanced down the street.

"No. It's a newspaper correspondent. That's my guess. The Washington and New York papers have had time to send special men here by now for feature stories."

The young man went briskly up the steps of No. 5.

"I was right," concluded Bristow. "If you run into him, chief, do the talking for the two of us. Just tell him I refuse to be interviewed."

"Why?" demanded Greenleaf. "An interview would give you good advertising."

"There's just one sort of publicity that's better

than talking," said Bristow laconically; "aloofness, mystery. It makes people wonder, keeps them talking."

It happened as Bristow had thought. Greenleaf, going down the walk, met the stranger, special correspondent of a New York paper. They had a short colloquy, the newspaper man looking frequently toward No. 9, and finally they turned and went down Manniston Road.

Bristow, leaving his chair to go back to the sleeping porch, saw Miss Kelly come out of No. 5 and hurry in his direction. He waited for her.

"Miss Fulton wants to see you, Mr. Bristow," said the nurse. "She asked me to tell you it's very important."

He was frankly surprised.

"Wants to see me, Miss Kelly?"

"Yes; at once, if you can come."

"Why, certainly."

He stepped into the house and got his hat.

"How is Miss Fulton?" he inquired, descending the steps with Miss Kelly.

"Much better. In fact, she seemed in good spirits and fairly strong as soon as her father and Mr. Withers left. That was about half an hour ago."

"Perhaps, their departure helped her," he suggested, smiling. "Often one's family is annoying —we may love them, but we want them at a lovable distance."

She gave him an approving smile.

"What about the medicine?" he asked as they

reached the door. "Has she had much bromide—stuff like that?"

"No; not today. Her mind's perfectly clear."

He put one more question:

"Do you happen to know why she wishes to see me?"

"I think it's something about her brother-in-law, Mr. Withers."

"Ah! I wonder whether——"

He did not finish the sentence, but, stepping into the living room, waited for Miss Kelly to announce his arrival.

The quick mechanism of his mind informed him that he was about to be confronted with some totally unexpected situation.

CHAPTER XVII

MISS FULTON'S REVELATION

PREPARED as he was for surprise, his emotion, when he was ushered into Miss Fulton's room, was little short of amazement. The girl was transformed. Instead of a spoiled child, with petulant expression, he beheld a calm, well controlled woman who greeted him cordially with a smile. Overnight, it seemed, she had developed into maturity.

Wearing a simple, pale blue negligée, and propped up in bed, as she had been the day before, she had now in her attitude nothing of the weakness she had shown during his former interview with her. For the first time, he saw that she was a handsome woman, and it was no longer hard for him to realize why Braceway had been in love with her. He waited for her to explain why he had been summoned.

"I've taken affairs into my own hands—that is, my affairs," she said. "There's something you should know."

"If there is anything——" he began the polite formula.

"First," she told him, "I'd better explain that father ordered me to discuss the—my sister's death with nobody except Judge Rogers. You know who he is, the attorney here. Father and

George have retained him. I haven't seen him yet. I wanted to give you certain facts. I know you'll make the just, proper use of them."

"Then I was right? You do know——"

"Yes," she said, exhibiting, so far as he could observe, no excitement whatever; "I was not asleep the whole of Monday night. I narrowly escaped seeing my sister die—seeing her murdered."

Her lips trembled momentarily, but she took hold of herself remarkably. A trifle incredulous, he watched her closely.

"I heard a noise in the living room. It wasn't a loud noise. The fact that it was guarded, or cautious, waked me up, I think. Before I got out of bed, I looked at my watch. It was somewhere in the neighbourhood of one o'clock—I'm not sure how many minutes after one. As I reached the little hallway opening into the dining room, I heard a man's voice.

"He was not talking aloud. It was a hurried sort of whisper. It seemed as if the voice, when at its natural pitch, would have been high or thin, more of a tenor than anything else. It gave me the impression of terriffic anger, anger and threat combined. The only thing I heard from my sister was a stifled sound, as if she had tried to cry out and been prevented by—by choking."

She looked out the window, her breast rising and falling while she compelled herself to calmness.

Bristow was looking at her with hawk-like keenness.

"And what did you do?" he asked, his voice low and cool.

"I pulled the dining room door open. From where I stood, looking across the dining room into the living room, I could see the edge of my sister's skirt and—and a man's leg, the right leg.

"That is, I didn't see much of his leg. What I did see was his foot, the sole of his shoe, a large shoe. He was in such a position that the foot was resting on its toes, perpendicular to the floor, so that I saw the whole sole of the rubber shoe."

She put both hands to her face and closed her eyes, holding the attitude for several minutes. When she looked at him again, there were no tears in her eyes, but the traces of fear.

"It seemed to me that he was leaning far forward, putting most of his weight on his left foot and balancing himself with the right thrust out behind him. There was something in the position of that leg which suggested great strength.

"All that came to me in a minute, in a second. When I realized what I saw, the danger to Enid, I fainted, just crumpled up and slid to the floor, and everything went black before me. I don't think I had made a sound since leaving the sleeping porch."

Bristow spoke quickly.

"Miss Fulton, who was the man?"

She overcame a momentary reluctance.

"I'm not sure," she said slowly. "I am not sure. I thought it was either Henry Morley or George Withers."

She turned away. A tremor shook her from head to foot.

"Why?" he asked.

"First, the voice," she replied, her face still averted. "It could so easily have been Mr. Morley's high voice lowered to a whisper; or it might have been George Withers'. When he's angry, his deep voice undergoes a curious change; it's horrid."

"And the second reason?"

"The man wore rubbers." She turned her face toward him. "I had seen Mr. Morley put his on two hours before that."

"How about your brother-in-law?"

"He's a crank on the subject—never goes out in the rain unless he has them on."

"Think a moment, Miss Fulton. Couldn't that man have been a negro—the negro who is now held for the crime? He wore rubber-soled shoes. Could you swear that what you saw was not a rubber sole attached to a leather or canvass shoe?"

"No; I couldn't."

"And the voice? Did you hear any of the man's words? Could you swear that it wasn't the illiterate talk of an uneducated negro?"

"No; I couldn't."

"What made you think of Morley and Withers?"

"Mr. Morley was in a raging temper with my sister when he left me—in connection with money matters. You know about that part of the affair?"

"Yes."

"And George's voice is always like the one I heard. It's like that when he gets—used to get—into a temper with Enid."

Bristow felt immensely relieved. He was so sure of his case against Perry Carpenter that he refused to consider anything tending to obscure his own theory.

"Are you still sure it was Mr. Morley or Mr. Withers?"

"I think now," she answered, her voice hardly above a whisper, "it was George Withers."

"Why?"

"Let me explain again. I lay there, where I had fainted, for hours, until just a few minutes before you answered my call for help. I must have had a terrific shock. When I recovered consciousness, I stumbled into the living room and saw—saw Enid. Her—oh, Mr. Bristow!—the sight of her face, of her mouth, paralyzed my voice.

"I stood on the porch and tried to scream, but at first I couldn't. I only gasped and choked. I started down the steps, reached the bottom, and then found I could make myself heard. I ran back up the steps and stood there shrieking until I saw you coming. I suppose nobody had seen me go down the steps."

"But that hasn't anything to do with Mr. Withers?"

"Yes—yes, it has. When I went down the porch steps, I saw something lying in the grass, on the upper side of the steps, the side toward your house."

She slipped her hand under one of the pillows.

"It was this."

She handed to Bristow an open-faced gold watch. He read on the back of it the initials, "G. S. W."

"It's George Withers' watch," she said, "and, when I found it, he had not been on this side of

Manniston Road, according to the story he told you and the chief of police."

Bristow was thinking intently, a frown creasing his forehead. He was wishing that she had not found the watch. He reminded himself of the hysterical condition she had been in the day before. Perhaps, after all, this story was nothing but an unconscious invention—a fantasy which she thought to be the truth.

"Why did you refuse yesterday to tell me this; and why do you volunteer it now?" he inquired, holding her glance with a cold, level look.

"I'm afraid you won't understand," she answered, a little smile lifting the corners of her mouth, a smile which, somehow, still had in it a great deal of sorrow. "Yesterday I was still under the influence of the way I had lived all my life, subjugated, as it were, by the fact that my older sister was my father's favourite and by the further fact that my sister's personality was stronger than mine—at least, I had been taught to think so.

"I don't want you to think I didn't love my sister. I did; but it made a cry-baby out of me. I always relied on others—do you see? But now, that influence is gone. I'm my own mistress; and I know it. I can and must do what strikes me as right."

Bristow, close student of human nature that he was, did understand. There flashed across his mind a passage he had read in something by George Bernard Shaw: that nobody ever loses a friend or relative by death without experiencing some measure of relief.

"Yes; I see what you mean," he assented; "its an instance of submerged personality—something of that sort."

"Mr. Braceway is working with you, isn't he?" she asked suddenly.

"Why, yes," he replied, surprised.

"I thought," she continued, "that what I had seen would be of service to you and him. And I can't understand why father and George want all this secrecy. One would think they were afraid of finding out something—something to make them ashamed! What I want is to see the guilty man punished—that's all."

He recalled Braceway's statement that he had been engaged to marry Maria Fulton. Could it be that she still loved him, and that the engagement to Morley, her helping him financially, had been all a pretense, the pitiful product of pique toward Braceway to show him she cared nothing for him? And now she wanted to help Braceway, not Bristow?

He decided to ignore that part of the situation. The obvious incrimination of Withers gave him enough to think about. He was sorry it had happened. He did not believe there was the shadow of a case against him.

He rose and handed the watch to Miss Fulton.

"No," she objected; "I don't want it. You and Mr. Braceway, perhaps, will make use of it."

He hesitated before putting it into his pocket.

"Why did you send for me, Miss Fulton?" he asked, after thanking her for doing so. "Why me instead of your lawyer, Judge Rogers?"

"He would have forbidden me to talk," she answered simply; "and I wanted to talk. I refuse ever again to carry around with me other people's secrets. It's too oppressive."

"Have you told this to anybody else?—or do you intend to?"

"No; nobody; and I won't."

"Now, one thing about Mr. Morley: do you think he has stolen money—from his bank, for instance?"

"Why, no! He was speculating—and losing. I'm glad you asked about him. I shall never see him again—never!"

Bristow left her with the assurance that he and Braceway would make the best possible use of her theory and the facts she had adduced. He walked slowly back to his bungalow, his limp more pronounced than usual. He felt physically very tired.

But of one thing he was still certain: the strength of his case against Perry Carpenter. He chose to stick to that, much more stubbornly than Braceway had refused to consider minutely the exact situation of Withers in regard to the crime. If Withers had murdered his wife, circumstances were now ideally in his favour. The two men, unusually brainy, quick thinkers, who were recognized by the police and the public as able to bring punishment on the guilty man, had other and opposing theories—theories which they were resolved to "put over," to substantiate. As matters stood now, the story Bristow had just heard was hardly a factor. The detectives were busy with ideas of their own.

Maria Fulton, after the lame man had left her,

lay back against her pillows and looked out the window with misty eyes. Counteracting the sorrow that had weighed upon her for two days, was her speculation as to how Braceway would receive the facts she had revealed.

Would he see that her course was one which she intended to be of help to him?—that, not knowing how he would treat a direct message from her, she had sent it to him through another?—that she desired, above all things, his success in the investigation?

"When I spoke to this man of Sam Braceway, my whole manner was a revelation of how I felt—a frank declaration! And, of course, he will tell him. If he doesn't——"

She called Miss Kelly.

CHAPTER XVIII

WHAT'S BRACEWAY'S GAME?

BRACEWAY, keeping his promise to have another conference with Bristow, sat on the porch of No. 9 and watched the last golden streamers the setting sun had flung above the blue edges of the mountains.

He still carried his cane.

"What's your plan now, Mr. Braceway?" Bristow inquired. "You think you'll follow Morley to Washington?"

"Not follow him," the detective answered smilingly. "I'm going with him. That is, I'll take the same train he does."

"Greenleaf told you, I suppose, that he'd given Morley permission to leave tonight?"

"Yes—said you suggested it. And I think you're right. There's no use in losing time unnecessarily. Are you going, too?"

"Oh, by all means," Bristow said quickly, "and against my doctor's orders. That is, if you don't object—if you don't think I'd be in the way."

Braceway was clearly aware of the lame man's desire to accompany him so as t obe associated with every phase of the work on the case, and to make it stand out emphatically in the long run that he, Bristow, pitting his ingenuity against Braceway, had gathered the evidence establishing the negro's guilt beyond question. The idea amused him, he was so sure of the accuracy of his own theory.

"Not at all," he said heartily. "I want you to come."

"How about avoiding him on the train? We don't want him to know we're his fellow-travellers."

"Oh, no. He'll get aboard at the station here. I have a machine to take me—and you, of course—to Larrimore, the station seven miles out. They'll flag the train. We'll get into a stateroom and stay there; have our meals served right there. You see, we don't get into Washington until dark tomorrow night."

"Yes; I see. The scheme's all right."

They were silent for several minutes.

"I've been thinking," said Bristow, "about Mrs. Withers having kept all her jewelry in the bungalow—unprotected, you know—nobody but her sister and herself there. It was risky."

"Yes," agreed Braceway. "What do you get from that?"

"Perhaps she was waiting—knew demands for money might come at any time—and was afraid to be caught without them."

"Exactly. That's the way I figured it."

They were silent again.

Braceway was the first to speak. He narrated all the facts he had learned from Abrahamson and Roddy, and concluded with the story Withers had told him on the station platform. He held back none of the details. Evidently, his irritation toward Withers had subsided. When Bristow handed him the watch Maria Fulton had found, he said laughingly:

"It's a good thing George told me about it, isn't it? Otherwise, we might have had to devote a lot of time to showing that he had nothing to do with the crime itself."

"And yet," qualified Bristow, "he said nothing to explain why the watch should have been so far back in the grass and to the side of the steps in this direction. According to his story, he must have dropped it on the other side, the down side."

"What do you mean?"

"I don't see how it could have fallen where Miss Fulton found it unless somebody had actually picked it up and thrown it there. He told you he was all the time down on the sidewalk, and, when the other man flung him off, he reeled down-hill, not up."

"That's hair-splitting," Braceway objected good-humouredly. "Nothing could make me think George responsible for the murder."

Bristow repeated then everything Maria Fulton had said that afternoon, and gave a fair, clear idea of her strong suspicion that the murder had actually been done by either Withers or Morley. It had no effect on Braceway.

"Miss Fulton," he said, "told you, of course, what she had seen and heard and, in addition, what she had guessed. But I don't see that is changes anything. I can't let it make me suspect Withers any more than I can accept as valuable Abrahamson's quite positive opinion that the man wearing the disguise was Withers. Things don't fit in. That's all. They don't fit into such a theory."

"Have you ever thought," persisted Bristow, "why Withers told Greenleaf and me yesterday morning that he was in the pawnshop when the man with the gold tooth was in there? Why should he say that when Abrahamson contradicts it at once by telling you they were at no time in the shop simultaneously?"

"Did Withers say to you outright, flat and unmistakably, that he saw the fellow inside the shop?" Braceway's voice had in it the ring of combativeness.

Bristow tried to remember the exact words Withers had used. Also, his harping on Withers' possible guilt struck him as absurd when he considered the strength of the case against Perry.

"I can't swear he did," he admitted at last; "but there's no doubt about the impression he gave us. Why, Abrahamson himself told you Greenleaf was positive Withers and the other man were there at the same time."

"Oh," Braceway said, obviously a little bored, "That's one of the things we have to watch for in these cases—wild impressions, the construing of words in a different way by everybody who heard them. It's a minor detail anyway."

"I don't get you at all," Bristow said, eyeing him intently.

"What do you mean?"

"Your conviction that Morley's the guilty man, your refusal to accept the case against Perry Carpenter, and your impatience in discussing Withers."

"Think over Miss Fulton's story," Braceway retorted. "If it does anything at all, it strengthens the suspicion that Morley's the man we want. And Roddy's story—on its face, it damns Morley! Withers had no motive except, a remote possibility, that of jealousy. Morley's motive was as old as time; the desperate need of money."

"Well, let's grant that, for the moment. What do you do with the evidence against the negro? He was after money."

Braceway laughed.

"To tell the truth," he admitted, "I don't do anything with it. I'll go further: it seems flawless, and yet——"

His face settled into serious lines.

"The report from the laboratory is unanswerable," Bristow went on. "It's as good as a statement from an eyewitness."

"Yes; it is. Still, in some way, I don't feel sure —But I'll say this: if my trip to Washington, our trip, isn't successful, I'll quit guessing and theorizing. I'll agree, without reservation, that Perry's the man."

Bristow hesitated before making his next remark:

"Of course, I'm not employed by Withers. My only connection with the case is a volunteer one. Yours is entirely different—and I realize that there may be—well—things you know and don't want me to know. But I can't help wondering whether Morley is the only consideration that takes you to Washington, whether there mightn't be something else relating, in a way, to the case—relating to it and yet not necessarily tied to it directly."

"What kind of something?" Braceway retorted.

"Say, for instance, something ugly, something painful to Fulton and Withers—terrific scandal, perhaps."

Braceway thought a moment.

"You've a keen mind, Mr. Bristow," he said finally. "I can't discuss that phase of it now, but you're partially right; although I'll say frankly, if Morley wasn't going to Washington, I wouldn't go either."

"Thanks; I appreciate your telling me that much. Now, let me ask one more question: why, exactly are you following Morley?"

"I'll tell you," Braceway replied with spirit. "It's a fair question, and I'll answer it. I'm going there on a hunch. I can't persuade myself that Perry's guilty, and I've a hunch that I'm now on the trail of the right man. And, as long as I'm in the business as a professional detective, I don't propose to disregard one scintilla of evidence, one smallest clue. I'll run down every tip and any hunch before I'll quit a case, saying virtually: 'Well, that man, or this man, *seems* guilty; go ahead and string him up.'

"No innocent man's going to his death as long as I feel there's a chance of the guilty fellow being around and laughing up his sleeve. That's the whole thing in a nutshell. That's why I'm after Morley! That's why I'm going to Washington."

Bristow, responding warmly to the other's voice and mood, leaned forward and grasped his hand.

"Good!" he said. "That's fine—and I'm with you."

"It's the only way to look at this work. Without the proper ideals, it's a rotten business. But, with the right viewpoint, it's great, at times far more valuable than the work of lawyers and judges."

"I'm glad you said that," Bristow declared; "very glad, because I'm thinking of going into it myself."

"You are?" Braceway appeared surprised; or his emotion might have been sympathy for a man driven to the choice of a new profession in life.

"Yes. I was talking about it to Greenleaf this afternoon. I realize—I'd be foolish if I didn't—that this case has given me a lot of publicity. It has put me where I can say I know something about crime and criminals, although, up until this murder, the knowledge has been mostly on paper."

"Yes; I know."

"But now, since I'm stuck down here for this long convalescence, it's the best thing I can do; in fact, it's the only thing. I've drifted through life fooling with real estate and writing now and then a little, a very little, poor fiction. Neither occupation would support me in Furmville; and I think I could make good as a sort of consulting detective and criminologist. There's money in it, isn't there?"

"Yes; good money," Braceway replied without much enthusiasm. "But there are times when it's heart-breaking work, this thing of running down the guilty, the scum of the earth, the failures, the rotters, and the rats. It isn't all a Fourth of July celebration with the bands playing and your name in the papers."

"Oh, I understand that. Any profession has its drawbacks."

"But you have the analytical mind. And, as I just said, there's money in it."

The glow had faded from the sky, and, with the darkness, there had come a noticeable chill in the air. Braceway yawned and stretched his arms. In addition to his talks with Abrahamson, Roddy, and Withers, he had also interviewed Perry and Lucy Thomas.

"By George!" he said explosively. "I'm tired. I don't know when I've been this tired. This has been a real day, something popping every minute since I got here this morning."

Bristow did not answer that. He was thinking of the impression he had received from Maria Fulton that she was still in love with Braceway. He had had that idea quite vividly while talking to her. He wondered now whether he had better mention it to Braceway. No, he decided; the time for that would come after the grinding work in Washington. Bristow himself was far from being a sentimental man. If he had been in Braceway's place, he would have preferred to hear nothing about the girl and her emotions until after the completion of the work.

"Are you packed up?" Braceway asked. "Ready to go?"

"Almost."

"Well, suppose we drift on down to the Brevord. No; I forgot. You'd rather drive down, wouldn't you? Walking would bother that leg. I'll send the machine up for you."

"Thanks," Bristow accepted appreciatively. "That will be best."

"All right. I'll have it up here in an hour or so. You can pick me up, and we'll run out to Larrimore."

He went down Manniston Road, his heels striking hard against the concrete. Under the light at the far corner he flashed into Bristow's vision, twirling his cane on his thumb; his erect, alert figure giving little evidence of the weariness he had felt a few minutes before.

The lame man lingered on the porch, considering Braceway's confident assertion that he did not "propose to disregard one scintilla of evidence, one smallest clue." But, he reflected, that was exactly what Braceway was doing: not only disregarding one scintilla, but keeping himself blind to a great many clues, the evidence against George Withers and that against the negro.

"I can't make out his game," he concluded. What's his idea about scandal, I wonder? The only possible scandal lies in the fact that Mrs. Withers paid blackmail for years. And the only way to make the fact public is to keep on denying that Perry's guilty. He seems to be trying to dig up scandal instead of hiding it."

Suddenly, with his characteristic quickness of thought, he realized that he disliked Braceway, definitely felt an aversion for him. When he was in Braceway's presence, influenced by his vitality and magnetism and listening to his conversation, he lost sight of his real feeling; but, left to himself, it came to the surface strongly. He wished he had never met the man. He knew he would never get close to him. And yet, he thought, why dislike him?

"Oh, he isn't my kind. *I* don't know. Yes, I know. He's just an edition de luxe of the ordinary four-flusher, a lot of biff-bang talk and bluff." He laughed, perhaps ridiculing himself. "Why waste mental energy on him? I've worked this case out. He hasn't."

And public opinion was with him. It conceded that he had the right answer to the puzzle. At that very moment the "star" reporter of *The Sentinel* was hammering out on his typewriter the following paragraph for publication in the morning:

"While it is generally recognized that Chief Greenleaf deserves great praise for the promptness with which the guilty man was discovered, the chief himself called attention this evening to the invaluable assistance he had received from Mr. Lawrence Bristow, already a well-known authority on crime. It was Bristow who, in addition to other brilliant work, forged the last and most impressive link in the chain of evidence against Carpenter. He did this by suggesting that the tests be made to determine whether or not the negro's finger nails showed traces of a white person's skin."

Later on in his story, the reporter wrote:

"Not a clue has yet been uncovered leading to the location of the stolen jewelry."

If Braceway could have read that, he would have

said: "Wait until we get to Washington. That's where we'll come across the jewels. Give us time."

Bristow, having a different opinion, would have refused to divulge it. The last thing he expected was any such result in Washington.

CHAPTER XIX

AT THE ANDERSON NATIONAL BANK

WHEN the train pulled into Washington at eleven o'clock, Henry Morley, the first passenger to alight, shook off the red-cap porters who grabbed at his grips, and hurried toward the gates. Braceway, well hidden by shadows just inside the big side-door of one of the baggage coaches, observed how pale and haggard he looked under the strong glare of the arc-lights.

"Hardly more than a kid!" thought the detective, with involuntary sympathy. "Why is it that most of the criminals are merely children? If they were all hardened and abandoned old thugs this work would be easier."

Nevertheless, he kept his eyes on Morley and, a moment later, moved a step forward. This made him visible to a well-dressed, sleek-looking man who up to that time had been standing on the dark side of the great steel pillar directly across the platform from the baggage car. Braceway, with a quick gesture, indicated the identity of Morley, and the sleek-looking man, suddenly coming to life, fell into the stream of street-bound passengers.

Braceway went back to the Pullman and rejoined Bristow, who was waiting for him in the stateroom.

In the taxicab on their way to the Willard Hotel, the lame man lay back against the cushion, apparently tired out and making no pretense of interest in anything. Braceway muttered something inaudible.

"What's that?" Bristow asked, opening his eyes.

"I'd been thinking what a pity it is that most criminals are youngsters. When you nab them, you feel as if they hadn't a fair show; it hardly seems a sporting proposition. After that, I soothed myself by considering the satisfaction one feels in landing the old birds, the ones who know better."

"I can appreciate that," the other agreed. "That may be one reason why I'm glad I've fastened the thing on an ignorant negro rather than on a fellow like Morley."

"You've too much confidence in circumstantial evidence, Bristow. I remember what an old lawyer once told me: 'Circumstantial evidence is like a woman, too tricky—and tells a different story every day.'"

At the Willard, finding that adjoining rooms were not to be had, they were put on different floors. Going toward the elevators, Braceway said:

"Unless something unexpected turns up, let's have breakfast at eight."

"And then, what?"

"Go to the Anderson National Bank. A man named Beale, Joseph Beale, is its president. We'll have to persuade him to have the records examined, to see how Morley stands. If he's wrong, short, the rest will be easy."

"Very good. Did your man pick him up at the train?"

"Oh, yes. Platt's always on the job. He and his partner, Delaney, generally deliver."

"Who are they?" Bristow asked, interested. "How do they happen to be working for you?"

"They belong to a private bureau here, Golson's. Golson and I have worked together before."

In the elevator Bristow was thinking that the matter of becoming a professional detective was not as simple as it had appeared to him. The work required colleagues, assistants, "shadowers," and reciprocal arrangements with bureaus in other cities. It was like any other profitable business, complicated, demanding constant attention.

When they met at breakfast, Braceway had already received Platt's report.

"Nothing developed last night," he told Bristow. "Platt followed Morley, who went straight to his home. He and his mother live in a little house far out on R Street northwest. Morley took the street car and was home by a little after half-past eleven. The lights were all out by a quarter past twelve. This morning at six-thirty, when Delaney relieved Platt, our man hadn't left the house."

"What's your guess about today?"

"Either he'll go to the bank on time this morning, to throw off suspicion," said Braceway, "or, if he mailed the jewelry to himself here the night of the murder, he'll try to pawn them in Baltimore or at a pawnshop in Virginia, just across the river. There are no pawnshops in Washington. There's a law that interferes."

"Delaney won't lose him?"

"Not a chance."

During the meal he saw that Bristow was completely worn out. As a matter of fact, he looked actually sick.

"See here," Braceway said as they were ready to leave the table; "you look all in, done out."

Bristow did not deny it.

"I didn't sleep very well last night. It was close in my room, and this morning the humidity's oppressive. You know what that does to us of the T. B. tribe."

"Suppose you get some more rest. It's going to be a sweltering day."

"Oh, I can stand it. I want to go with you. I'm not going to feel any worse than I do now."

But the other was insistent. Bristow at last gave in. He would take the rest if Braceway would report progress to him at noon.

Returning to his room, the sick man swore savagely.

"Friday!" he said aloud. "Damn it all anyway!"

Braceway lingered several minutes on the steps outside the Anderson National Bank. He felt reluctant to go inside and start the machinery that would ruin Morley. It wasn't absolutely necessary, he argued, with something like weakness; he could, perhaps, find out all he wanted to know without——

He thought suddenly of the bizarre performances of the thing men call Fate. Because a woman is murdered under mysterious circumstances in a little southern city, evidence is uncovered showing that a panic-stricken boy has been stealing money from a bank hundreds of miles away; a detective is employed by the dead woman's husband; the detective is thrown again into contact with the victim's sister and realizes more clearly than ever that he loves her.

What would be the result of it all—the result for him? He remembered the gown she had worn to a ball, something of the palest yellow—how the blue of her eyes and the gleam of her hair had been emphasized by the simple perfection of the gown. What would she say if he went back to——

He forced himself down to reality.

He entered the bank and discovered that Morley had not reported for work. Having presented his card to a chilly, monosyllabic little man, he was shown, after a short wait, into a private office where, surrounded by several tons of mahogany, Mr. Joseph Beale reigned supreme.

Mr. Beale struck him as a fattened duplicate of Mr. Illington, thin of lip, hard of eye, slow and precise in enunciation. In spite of his stoutness, he had the same long, slender fingers, easy to grasp with, and the same mechanical Punch-and-Judy smile. When he greeted the detective, his voice was like a slow, thin stream that had run over ice.

"I'm not on a pleasant mission, Mr. Beale,"

Braceway began. "It's something in the line of duty."

The bank president looked at the card which had been handed to him.

"Ahem!" he said, with a lip smile. "You're a detective?"

"Yes."

"Well, Mr. Braceway, what is it? Let's see whether I can do anything for you. At least, I assume you want——"

This ruffled Braceway.

"I want nothing," he said crisply; "and I'm afraid I'm going to do something for you."

The banker stiffened.

"What is it?"

"It's one of your employés; in fact, it's your receiving teller."

"What! Henry Morley! Impossible, sir! Outrageous! Preposterous!"

"Just a moment, if you please," put in Braceway. "I was going to say that I was positive about nothing. I've been compelled to suspect, however, that Mr. Morley might be short in his accounts. There are unexplained circumstances which seem to connect Mr. Morley with the murder of a woman. Therefore——"

"One of the—one of my employés a thief and a murderer!" Mr. Beale pushed back his chair and fell to patting his knees with his fists. "Great God, Mr. ——" He looked at the card again. "Why, Mr. Braceway, I can't believe it. It would be treason to this bank, treason to all its traditions!" He had not suffered such an attack of garrulity for the past twenty years. "And Morley, his family, his birth! By George, sir, his blood! Are we to lose all faith in blood?"

"As I wanted to say," Braceway managed to break in, "the murder of Mrs. George S. Withers in Furmville, North Carolina, led——"

This was the crowning blow. Mr. Beale gasped several times in rapid succession, not entirely hiding his slight, cold resemblance to a fish.

"Mrs. Withers!" he got out at last. "The daughter of my old friend, Will Fulton! Fulton, one of our depositors!"

He was reduced to silent horror.

Braceway took advantage of his condition and outlined the circumstances in considerable detail.

"If he's short in his accounts," he concluded, "the motive for the murder is established. And, if he's been stealing from the bank, you want to know it."

Mr. Beale pushed a bell-button.

"Charles," he said to the chilly little man, "tell Mr. Jones I want to speak to him. Our first vice-president," he explained to Braceway.

Mr. Jones, evidently dressed and ready for the part of president of the bank whenever Mr. Beale should see fit to die, came in and, with frowns, "dear-dears" and tongue-clucking, heard from the president the story of what had befallen the Anderson National.

"How soon," inquired Beale, "can we give this—er—gentleman an answer, a definite answer, as to whether Morley, the unspeakable scoundrel, is a thief?"

Mr. Jones considered sadly.

"Perhaps, very soon; two o'clock or something like that—and again it may take time to find anything. Suppose we say five or half-past five this afternoon; to be safe, you understand. Half-past five?"

"Very well," agreed Beale, and turned to Braceway: "Will that be satisfactory?"

"Perfectly."

Braceway left them, their mask-like faces plainly damaged by anxiety; their cool, slow utterance slightly humanized by the realization that they must act at once. In fact, as the detective closed the door of the private office, Mr. Jones was reaching with long, slender fingers for the telephone. They would need the best accountant they could find for the quick work they had promised Braceway.

CHAPTER XX

THE DISCOVERY OF THE JEWELS

BRACEWAY returned to the lobby of his hotel, and, having bought half a dozen New York newspapers, settled down to wait for a report from Golson's bureau concerning Morley's movements. A little after eleven he was called to the telephone.

"Your man caught the eight o'clock train for Baltimore." Golson himself gave the information. "Delaney also caught it. They got to Baltimore at nine. Your man took a taxi straight to the shop of an old fellow named Eidstein, reaching there at twenty minutes past nine. He and Eidstein went into Eidstein's private office back of the shop and stayed there for over an hour, in fact until about half-past ten. Your man came out and went to a down-town hotel. He was there when Delaney, still sticking to him, managed to get a wire to me telling me what I've just told you."

"Fine!" said Braceway. "What was he doing in the hotel? Did he meet anybody, or write anything?"

"Delaney didn't say."

"Who's this Eidstein, a pawn broker?"

"No; he's a dealer in antiques: furniture, old gold, old jewels, anything old. He stands well over there. He's all right. I know all about him."

"That's funny, isn't it?"

"What's funny?"

"That he didn't go to a pawnshop."

"Keep your shirt on," laughed Golson. "The day's not over yet."

"No doubt about that. What about Corning, the loan-shark in Virginia?"

"I've got a man over there, just as you asked. Shall I keep him on?"

"Sure!" snapped Braceway. "Suppose Morley gives Delaney the slip in Baltimore and doubles back to Corning's! Keep him there all day."

He left the telephone and went up to Bristow's room, No. 717. When he knocked, the door was opened by a young woman in the uniform and cap of a trained nurse.

"I beg your pardon," he began. "I got the wrong room, I'm afraid. I——"

"This is Mr. Bristow's room," she said in a low tone. "Are you Mr. Braceway?"

"Yes."

"Come in, then, please." She stepped back and held open the door. "Mr. Bristow's still very weak, but he told me to let you in. He said he must see you as soon as you arrived."

Braceway saw that there was no bed in the room, and asked where the sick man was. The nurse pointed to a closed door leading into the adjoining room.

"What's the matter with him?" he asked. "By George! He hasn't had a hemorrhage, has he?"

"Yes, sir. That's exactly what he has had. The

doctor says all he needs now is rest. He doesn't think there's any real danger. Will you go in to see him?"

She quietly opened the door to the sickroom. Braceway went in on tiptoes, but Bristow stirred and turned toward him when the nurse put up the window shade.

"You'll have to lie still, Mr. Bristow," she cautioned on her way out. "It's so important to keep these ice-packs in place."

"Thanks, Miss Martin; I shall get on," he answered in a voice so weak that it startled Braceway.

"I don't think you'd better talk," said his visitor. "Really, I wouldn't."

Bristow gave him a wry smile.

"It's nothing serious; just a—pretty bad hemorrhage," he said, finding it necessary to pause between words. "The boneheaded Mowbray—my physician in Furmville, you know—was right for once. He said—this might happen."

"I'm going out and let you sleep," Braceway insisted, displaying the average man's feeling of absolute helplessness in a sickroom.

"No, not yet. The fellow I had in—knows his business—put ice on the lung and on my heart—gave me something to lessen the heart action."

"And you're not in pain?"

"No. I'll be all right in—in a little—One thing I wanted to—tell you. Quite important—really."

He mopped his forehead with tremulous, futile little dabs which accentuated his weakness. Braceway instinctively drew his chair closer to the bed so as to catch all of the scarcely audible words.

"Just occurred to me," the sick man struggled on, "just—before I had this hemor—Ought to have somebody, extra man, working with Platt and Delaney. Tell you why: if Morley mailed the jewelry that—night of the murder, he wasn't fool—enough to mail it to himself or to his own—house. If he visits anybody today—we ought to have an extra man with Delaney. Delaney can keep on Morley's trail—extra man can watch and—if necessary, question anybody Morley visits or consults with. Then——"

"Correct!" exclaimed Braceway. "Right you are! Who says you're sick? Why, your bean's working fine. Don't try to talk any more. I'm going out to get busy on that very suggestion."

"Another thing," Bristow said, lifting a feeble hand to detain his visitor. "Come up here at six—this evening, will you? I'll have my strength back by that time. Don't laugh. I will. I know I will. I've had hemorrhages before this."

"What do you want to do at six?"

"Help you—be with you when you question Morley. Promise me. I'll be in shape by that time."

Braceway promised, and went into the outer room.

"Do you think," he asked Miss Martin, "there's the slightest chance of his getting up this evening, or tonight?"

"I really don't know," she smiled. "There may be. It all depends on his courage, his nerve. Anyway, he won't be able to do much, to exert himself."

"He's got the nerve," Braceway said admiringly; "got plenty of it. By the way, how did it happen? How do you happen to be here?"

"It seems that at about a quarter to ten Mr. Bristow called the downstairs operator and asked her to send a bellboy to his room, number seven-seventeen. When the boy came in here, Mr. Bristow was lying across the foot of his bed, pressing to his mouth a towel that was half-saturated with blood.

"He had dropped his saturated handkerchief on the bathroom floor. And he evidently had been bleeding when he was at the telephone. He was awfully weak, so weak that the boy thought he was dying. He couldn't speak. The boy remembered having seen the house physician, Dr. Carey, at a late breakfast in the café, and got him up here at once. Dr. Carey called me to take the case as soon as he had seen Mr. Bristow.

"I think that's all. Of course, the bed that was in here and all the other soiled things had been removed by the time I came in; and the management insisted on his taking the extra room."

"Thank you," said Braceway. "I'm glad to get the details. You'll see that he has everything he needs, won't you?"

A few minutes later, when Miss Martin entered the bedroom to lower the window shade, Bristow told her:

"I think I'll sleep now. Shut the door and, on no account, let—anybody, doctor or anybody else—

wake me up. You call me at six, please. What time is it now? Twelve-fifteen? Remember, you'll let me sleep? "

Braceway went to his own room to brush up for lunch. Although he had not taken the trouble to tell Bristow, he had already arranged with Golson to have the " extra man " on the job. He was taking no chances. He smiled when he thought of the sick man's eagerness to give him advice.

It occurred to him that he should have communicated with George Withers. The funeral was over; had been set for yesterday. He would send him a wire as soon as he went downstairs.

" By George! " Braceway communed with himself. " If I hadn't been his friend, I probably would have worried him. Even if Morley has embezzled from the bank, how closely have I coupled him with the crime? Not very closely unless he tries to pawn, or produces, some of the stolen stuff—not any more closely than George has coupled himself with it! George acted like such an ass! "

He was about to leave the room when, for the first time, he looked the situation squarely in the face and made an important acknowledgment to himself. There had been in his mind, ever since that train had pulled out of Furmville with George's rattling whisper still sounding in his ear, the desire and the plan to safeguard George. He had felt, on this trip, that, if his theory about the case broke down, it might be advisable, even necessary, to produce all the evidence possible to shield his friend either from ugly gossip or from the downright charge of murder. He did not believe for a moment that Withers was guilty.

If things went wrong in the next eight or ten hours, if it was proved that Morley had nothing to do with the murder, the thing he wanted above all else was a story from Morley that he, Morley, had seen the struggle in front of No. 5 as Withers had described it. Somehow, that story about the struggle had struck him as the weakest link in George's whole story.

He had resolutely refused to consider it up to now, but he no longer could dodge it. He had come to Washington to catch the criminal. But he also had come with the subconscious plan of getting at anything that would help Withers.

He stood for an instant, jangling the room key in his hand. A frown drew his brows together. The frown deepened. He unlocked the door, went back into the room, and put down his cane, leaning it against the wall near the bureau.

He reached the lobby in time to hear a callboy paging him. There was a telegram for him. It read:

"Mr. S. S. Braceway, Willard Hotel, Washington, D. C.

"Here.

(Signed) "Frank Abrahamson."

"What the devil does he mean?" he asked himself several times. "What's this 'here' about?"

He thought a long time before he remembered having asked the Furmville pawn broker to try to recall where he had seen the bearded man in another disguise, a disguise which, apparently, had consisted of nothing but a black moustache and bushy eyebrows. And Abrahamson had promised to wire him if he did remember. The "here" meant it was in Furmville that he had seen the moustached man.

He went to the telegraph desk and wrote out a message:

"Mr. Frank Abrahamson, 329 College Street, Furmville, N. C.

"Silence.

(Signed) "Braceway."

"One-word telegrams!" he smiled grimly. "Thrifty fellows, these chosen people."

He found the telephone booths and called up Golson.

"Got anything from Baltimore?" he inquired.

"Just been talking to Delaney on long-distance," Golson answered without enthusiasm.

"Well! What is it?"

"Your man gave him the slip a quarter of an hours ago, and he wants——"

"Gave him the slip!" shouted Braceway. "What are you talking about?"

"I don't like it any more than you do," snapped Golson. "But that's what happened: gave him the slip."

"How?"

"I didn't get that exactly. Delaney merely said he lost him in the hotel. Your man was evidently waiting there for a message or phone call. If he received it, Delaney was fooled. Anyway, he's gone now; and Delaney wants to know what he's to do. What'll I tell him?"

"Tell him to go to hell!" Braceway said hotly. "No! Tell him to go back to Eidstein's and wait there until Morley shows up. That's his only chance to pick him up again."

"O. K.," growled Golson.

"Say! Put somebody on the job of watching for the incoming trains from Baltimore, will you? Right away?"

"Platt's just come into the office. I'll send him to the station at once."

"What time did Delaney lose sight of Morley?"

"Twelve forty-five."

Braceway hung up the receiver and looked at his watch. It was ten minutes past one. He had fifty minutes to kill before keeping an appointment he had made with Major Ross, chief of the Washington police.

After a quick lunch, he strolled over to the newsstand and picked up the early edition of an afternoon paper.

The first headlines he saw were:

STOLEN GEMS FOUND
IN SUSPECT'S YARD

Under these lines was a dispatch from Furmville giving the information that plain-clothes men of the Furmville police force had discovered the emerald-and-diamond lavalliere worn by Mrs. Enid Fulton Withers the night she was murdered. The jewelry had been found in the yard of the house where Perry Carpenter had lived. The lavalliere was concealed in tall grass immediately beneath the window of Carpenter's room, and thus had at first escaped the eyes of the police. When found, it was intact except for the six links that had been broken from the chain and dropped the night of the murder.

Braceway threw down the paper and went to the Pennsylvania Avenue door.

"Damn!" he addressed mentally the top of the Washington monument. "More grist for Bristow's mill! I'm not crazy, am I? I'm not that crazy, that's sure!"

He set out to keep his appointment with Major Ross. After all, he felt reasonably sure of himself, and he had made up his mind to carry things through as he originally had intended. His shoulders were well back, his step elastic and quick. He flung off discouragement as if it had been an overcoat too warm for that weather.

He would not permit Delaney's fiasco to annoy him. The Baltimore police had been tipped to watch the pawnshops; Delaney probably would pick Morley up again; and there was the extra man yet to be heard from. Besides, Morley would break down and confess cleanly after his fright on being arrested. Things were not so bad after all.

CHAPTER XXI

BRISTOW SOLVES A PROBLEM

MR. BEALE and Mr. Jones were, so far as their exteriors showed, nearly back to the normal iciness of their every-day appearance when Braceway found them in the president's office a few minutes after half-past five. He did not have to ask what they had discovered; their faces were frank confessions. He dropped into a chair and smiled.

"How much?"

Mr. Beale cleared his throat and moved his lips deliberately one against the other.

"Before I say anything else, Mr.—er—Braceway, I want to express to you not only my own gratitude but that of all the officers and directors of the Anderson National. You have, it seems, saved us from great trouble. As things are, they are bad enough. But you have enabled us to put our fingers on the—ah—situation almost in time."

He glanced at Jones.

"Briefly," the vice-president took up the statement, "it has been established, thus far, that Morley has stolen from the Anderson National the—"

Mr. Beale's composure broke down at this. He interrupted the subordinate's calm explanation:

"Stolen from the Anderson National! Think

of that, sir! Of all the outrageous things, of all the unqualifiedly and absolutely incredible things! We have in our bank, on our payrolls, a thief, an unmitigated scoundrel!" He pushed back his chair and drummed on his knees. "We find that one of his thefts was seven hundred dollars, and another five hundred. We—I—trusted him, trusted him! And with what result?"

He slid his chair forward and bruised his fist by striking the desk with all his strength.

"And the crudity of his methods! Preposterous! The old trick of entries in pass-books and no entries in the records! He chose, for his own safety, depositors who carried large balances and were not apt to draw out anywhere near their total balance. It's the most abominable——"

Between the outbursts of the president and the cold, lifeless words of the vice-president, Braceway managed to elicit these facts: they expected to uncover more than the $1,200 shortage already established; when they could examine all the pass-books now out of the bank, the total would undoubtedly be found much larger; they demanded Morley's arrest at once; in fact, if the law had allowed it, they would have sent him to the scaffold within the next hour.

"Now," the detective reminded them, "he's also under suspicion of murder."

"My God!" spluttered Beale. "What do we care about murder? Hasn't he tried to murder this bank? Hasn't he assassinated, so far as he could, its good name? Get him! Put him behind the bars!"

At last they agreed to Braceway's plan: Morley was to be arrested by one of Major Ross' plain-clothes men when he stepped off the train from Baltimore. It was to be done quietly, so that the news of it would not be in the morning's papers.

He was then to be taken to one of the outlying police stations for the sake of privacy, was to be told that he was charged with embezzlement; and then, having been frightened by the arrest, he would be compelled to undergo the cross-examination of Braceway and Bristow, who wanted to prove or disprove his connection with the murder in Furmville.

Braceway returned to the hotel to await a report from either Major Ross or Delaney.

Delaney came into the lobby and joined him. They went straight to Braceway's room.

"We caught the five o'clock in Baltimore and got here a little before six," the big man started his story. "One of the men from headquarters stepped up to him and arrested him. I figured you had arranged for it, so I beat it up here."

"What happened in Baltimore?" asked Braceway in a tone so friendly that it dissipated much of the other's embarrassment.

"I declare, Mr. Braceway," he said humbly, "I don't know how it happened. I never had such a thing hit me before. But I lost him slick as a whistle. I was in the bar of the hotel, and he was sitting in the lobby. I had my eye right on him, and he had no idea I was following him. Then, all at once, after I'd turned to the barkeeper just long enough to order a soft drink, I looked around, and he was gone. I combed the house from top to bottom, but it was no use. He had ducked me clean."

"What time was that?"

"Twelve-forty-five."

"And then what?"

"The chief gave me your message, and I went back to keep a look on Eidstein's place. I didn't think he'd show there again, but he did—at four o'clock and stayed there almost half an hour. After that, he went to the station, me right after him. We both caught the five o'clock for Washington."

"Did you talk with Eidstein?"

"No, sir; had no orders. But he's no loan-shark, and no fence. Eidstein's on the level. We know all about him."

"How did Morley look when he showed up there the second time?"

"Done up, sir, fagged out. That's what makes me uneasy. He'd been up to something that shook him, something that rattled his teeth. He looked it."

"Pawning something, perhaps?"

"That's just it—just the way I figured it—something he knew was risky—something that made him sweat blood."

"Well, it's all right," Braceway concluded. "There's nothing for you to worry about. It may be that losing him was the best thing you ever did. I'm not sure, but it may turn out so."

Delaney, greatly relieved, thanked him and left.

Braceway hurried to the sick man's room and, having been ushered in by Miss Martin, found him, fully dressed, sitting on the edge of the bed. He was still pale and looked tired, but his voice was strong. He was setting down a half-empty glass of water on a tray near the bed, and his hand, although it wavered a little, had lost the helpless tremulousness Braceway had noticed at noon.

"Hello!" said the visitor. "You're a wonder! I expected to find you prostrated."

"Oh, no," Bristow answered quietly. "I knew the rest and sleep would bring me around all right, and Miss Martin has given me a twentieth of a grain of strychnine. What's the news?"

"I'll sketch it to you. But how about dinner?"

"I've arranged for us to have it up here, if you don't mind?"

Braceway agreed, and Miss Martin straightened up the other room, where the meal was served.

Bristow, restricting himself to clam broth, crackers, and coffee, heard the story of the day's developments with profound interest. Except for the little tremor in his fingers, there was no sign that he had been ill a few hours earlier. Not a detail escaped him. The whole thing was photographed on his mind, even the hours and minutes of the time at which this or that had occurred.

"So," concluded Braceway, "you can see why I feel pretty fine! Morley's a thief, as I'd believed all along. The motive for the murder is established, particularly when you remember that Miss Fulton, who had been advancing him money, was prevented by her sister from doing so any further."

"No; I can't see that," objected Bristow. "A motive? Yes; but not a motive for murder. So far as I can size it up, he wanted to steal more money, and that's all. It's a far cry between theft and murder."

"You stick to your old theory, the negro's guilt?"

"Naturally. There you have the motive and the murder—the proof that he said he would rob, and the indisputable evidence that he did rob and kill. Why, he brought away with him particles of the victim's body! What more do you want?"

For a long moment their glances interlocked and held. In a sharp, intuitive way Braceway felt that Bristow suspected his concern about George Withers. He did not know why he suspected it, but he did. He was convinced that the other, with his darting, analytical mind, had gone to the secret unerringly.

"Oh, well," he laughed, rising from the table, "if you're so fond of your own ideas, Bristow, you won't be of much use to me in questioning Morley tonight."

"On the contrary," the other returned quickly, "I'm just as anxious as you are to get the truth out of him. As long as one man's story is left vague and indefinite, just that long you run the risk of somebody's coming forward with facts or conjectures to overthrow the theory you've advanced. It applies to my idea as well as to yours."

"No doubt."

"You know as well as I do," the lame man continued, "that, if Perry Carpenter isn't guilty, the next one to suspect logically is Withers."

“What makes you say that?” The question was put sharply.

“I've two reasons. In the first place, the facts and Withers' own story; in the second, common sense.”

The telephone rang. When Bristow answered it, a man's voice asked for Braceway. Major Ross himself was on the wire.

“I had the man in Baltimore interviewed,” he reported. “Here is his story in a few words: some years ago Morley's father bought from his shop a pair of earrings, each one set with an unusually valuable pigeon's-blood ruby, and gave them to Mrs. Morley. Young Morley, now in trouble, took him this morning the two stones and asked him to buy them back. He explained that it must be done secretly because he might be suspected of having been implicated in a murder.

“He denied any guilt, but said it would embarrass him if the deal became known. The owner of the shop—you understand who—could not buy them back, but promised to raise money on them, something he'd never done before. He was greatly affected by Morley's grief and despair. He says the rubies are the ones he sold years ago.”

“Did he raise the money?”

“He tried, but couldn't get the sum Morley wanted, seven hundred dollars. Finally, he did advance it from his own pocket.”

“And the stones? How do they compare with those on the list of Withers' stuff?”

“Identical.”

“[illegible] right; thanks. We'll see you at eight.”

motive?

Braceway repeated the report to Bristow, eliciting the comment:

"Is somebody trying to make fun of us—or what is it? If those rubies belonged to Mrs. Withers, one thing at least is certain: Morley was in the bungalow the night of the murder, and after the murder had been committed. Miss Fulton distinctly told me the only jewelry that had ever passed between her and Morley was the ring found in his room in the Brevord that morning."

Braceway laughed aloud.

"At last," he said, "You're beginning to see the light—or to appreciate the jungle we're running around in."

He had arranged for them to meet Major Ross at the station house of No. 7 police precinct. Since it was off the principal beats of police reporters, Morley was detained there.

Bristow went into his bedroom, where Miss Martin gave him another dose of strychnine. He asked her to await his return—not that he expected to be in need of her, he said, but just to be on the safe side. He waved aside Braceway's solicitousness about his strength.

As they stepped into the corridor, a boy handed Braceway a telegram. He read it, and, without a word, handed it to Bristow. It said:

"Two diamonds and two emeralds, unset, apparently part of Withers jewelry, pawned here about two-thirty this afternoon by medium-sized man; a little slim; black moustache; high, straight nose; bushy eyebrows; very thin lips; gray eyes;

age between thirty and forty; weight 140 pounds. Two pawnshops used. No trace of him yet."

It was signed by the chief of the Baltimore plain-clothes force.

"What do you think of that?" asked Braceway, his voice hard.

"This Morley," answered Bristow, his voice equally hard, "must have lost his mind."

They went down and took a cab.

"That description," the lame man was thinking, as they rolled through the streets toward the northwest part of the city, "fits Withers perfectly, except for the moustache and the colour of the eyes. But that's absurd. I'd like to——"

He began again to wonder what, in addition to the capture of the guilty man, had brought Braceway to Washington. With his highly sensitized brain, he had received the impression that there was joined to the case some event or interest of which he had not the slightest inkling. How was Morley hooked up with the hidden phase of the affair? He intended to know all they knew about the whole business.

If Morley knew the secret—there was Maria Fulton! Incredulous for a moment, he considered an entirely new idea. His incredulity vanished—and he knew!

He lay back against the cab cushion and laughed, silently. His mirth grew. His laughter was almost beyond control. This was the thing that had bothered him, the "hidden angle" that had escaped him. He laughed until he shook. He had to put his hand to his mouth to prevent bursting into prolonged, riotous guffaws.

That was it—Withers and Fulton, and Braceway of course, were afraid of Morley, afraid of what he might say; not about events of the night of the murder, but what he might reveal concerning——

He struggled again with his consuming mirth. He saw now that he had handled everything exactly as it should have been handled.

Now, more than ever before, he was interested in what the embezzler would say under their examination and cross-questioning. It was like a game in which he, Bristow, was the assured winner before even the first move was made. He knew already the very thing they were so intent on concealing.

CHAPTER XXII

A CONFESSION

BRISTOW, satisfied now that he had fathomed Braceway's reluctance to accept as final the case against Perry Carpenter, had not been the only one mystified by the detective's course. Practically every other detective and police official in the country was wondering what secret motive had impelled Braceway to keep public attention focused on the tragedy after a flawless case against the real murderer had been established.

They knew that he was in the employ of the husband and father of the murdered woman, and that, therefore, his acts had the endorsement of her family. What, then, they asked, was the true situation back of the pursuit and persecution of the bank clerk, Henry Morley?

What possible interest could they have in running him down, in ruining his standing? What contingency was powerful enough to compel their approval of Braceway's forcing the conclusion upon the mind of the public that an ugly scandal had touched Mrs. Withers?

And this question, at first whispered in the gossip in Furmville, had crept into the newspaper dispatches. The result was a morbid curiosity generally, and, in the minds of many, a belief that

Braceway would fasten the crime on Morley. There were, however, a few who took the position that Morley, even if he had not committed the murder, had knowledge of some fact or facts even more terrible than the crime itself.

Major Ross awaited the two men in a large, bare-walled room on the second floor of the station house. The night was oppressively warm, and the tall, narrow windows were thrown open. Like Braceway, Bristow took off his coat, the absence of it showing plainly the outline of his heavy belt and steel brace.

Morley was ushered in and given one of the plain, straight-backed chairs with which the room was furnished. The only other furniture was a deal table, behind which Braceway, Bristow, and Major Ross sat in lounging attitudes. The major, aside from his interest in the case, was there merely as a matter of courtesy, a compliment to Braceway's reputation.

The prisoner, a few feet from them across the table, was suggestive of neither resistance nor mental alertness. Above his limp collar and loosened cravat, his face looked haggard and drawn. It was without a vestige of colour save for the blue shadows under his eyes. There was a tremor on his lips almost continuously.

Once or twice throughout the whole interview, his eyes brightened momentarily with a hint of cunning or attempted cunning. Except for these few flashes, he was manifestly beaten, unnerved, suffering from a simultaneous desire and inability to weigh and ponder what he said.

Braceway began, in quick, incisive sentences:

" You're up against it, Morley. You know it as well as we do. And we don't want to trick you or bully you. We're only after the truth. If you'll tell the truth, it will help you and us. Will you give us a straight story?"

" Yes," he answered dully, his hands folded, like a woman's, against his body.

Braceway put more imperiousness into his voice.

" You know you're under arrest for embezzlement, don't you?"

" Yes."

" And you did take money from the Anderson National Bank?"

Morley squirmed and looked at each of the three in front of him before he replied to that.

" Yes," he said finally, swallowing hard, his voice high and strained.

" Good! That's the sensible way to look at it," Braceway jogged him with rapid speech. " We needn't bother any more about that tonight. How about the jewelry you pawned in Baltimore today?"

The prisoner licked his lips and fixed on Braceway a look that grew into a stare.

" You mean the rubies?"

" Well, yes."

" I didn't pawn them, and—and they were my mother's."

" How about the diamonds and emeralds?"

" I had no diamonds and emeralds."

" You didn't! Where were you all the afternoon preceeding the time you showed up at Eidstein's?"

This was his first intimation that he had been watched. He hesitated.

"Do I have to tell that?"

"Certainly. Why shouldn't you?"

A film, like tears, clouded his weak eyes. His voice was disagreeably beseeching.

"It would bring my mother into this," he objected, twining his fingers about each other and shuffling his feet.

"You'll have to tell us where you were and what you did," Braceway persisted.

"Oh, very well," he said desperately; "I was in a room in the Emerson Hotel with—with my mother. And I was—I was confessing to her that I'd stolen from the bank. She knew I needed money. I had told her I'd been speculating, and needed some extra money for margins. She gave me the rubies from her earrings; and she followed me to Baltimore. If I couldn't raise the money on the rubies, she was to borrow it on our house. She owns that."

He paused, on the verge of tears.

"Buck up!" Braceway prodded him. "You confessed to her, did you?"

"Yes. At the last, somehow, I couldn't stand the idea of her giving up the last thing she had, but —but she would have done it."

"Could she have mortgaged her home in Baltimore?"

"Yes. Mr. Taliaferro, A. G. Taliaferro, the

lawyer, would have fixed it for her. He's a friend of the family—used to be of father's."

"Now, about the emeralds and diamonds?" Braceway began another attack.

"I don't know what you mean."

"They belonged to Mrs. Withers."

Morley shook his head impatiently.

"I don't know anything about them."

Bristow took a hand in the questioning, flicking him and provoking him by tone and word. But neither he nor Braceway could get an admission, or any appearance of admission, that he knew anything about the Withers jewelry.

Furthermore, he declared that his presence in the hotel, from the time Delaney had "lost" him until his second appearance at Eidstein's at four o'clock, could be established by the room clerk, two bellboys, and a maid at the Emerson, and by the lawyer, Taliaferro, with whom he had talked on the telephone while there with his mother.

According to him, he had unwittingly evaded Delaney by the simple act of stepping into the elevator and going to the room where his mother, having reached Baltimore an hour later than he, was waiting to hear how he had fared in his interview with Eidstein.

He had hoped, he said, to cover up the $700 shortage at the bank with the money obtained from the dealer in antiques, but, thinking of the risk of his mother's being impoverished, he had renounced at the last moment the plan of getting more money through the mortgage or sale of the home.

"Do you happen to know that a man, clumsily

disguised and answering to your description, pawned some of the Withers jewelry in Baltimore today?" Braceway asked.

"Did he?" He looked blank.

"Yes. What do you know about it?"

"I've already told you: not a thing."

Braceway, recognizing the futility for the present of prolonging this line of inquiry, paused, looking at him thoughtfully.

"If I pawned them," Morley added, without raising his eyes, "why wasn't the money found on me?"

"Don't get too smart!" Bristow put in so roughly and suddenly that the prisoner started violently. "What we want is facts, not arguments!"

The lame man leaned forward in his chair and made his voice sharp, provocative.

"You're not as clever as you think you are. You lied when you made your statement about the night Mrs. Withers was murdered. Now, come through with that—the truth about it!"

Morley, utterly bewildered, stared and said nothing.

"What did you do that night? Where were you?"

Bristow left his chair and, going round the table, stood in front of Morley.

"I told you that once. I wasn't anywhere near Manniston Road."

"Yes, you were! We've got proof of it. You *were* there!"

"What proof?"

"You're curious about that, are you? I thought

you would be! For one thing, the imprint of your rubber shoe on the porch floor of Number Five—"

"No! No! I wasn't on the porch. I——" He checked the words, realizing that he had betrayed himself.

"Not on the porch?" Bristow caught him up. "Where, then? Where?" He limped a step nearer to the prisoner. "Out with it now! You *were* there! You were there!"

He stood over Morley, conquering him by the sheer weight of his personality.

"I wasn't on the porch."

"All right—not on the porch. But where?"

Morley looked up at him and, mechanically, pushed his chair back, as if he felt the need of more space. Bristow, in his shirt-sleeves, his right arm held up, continued to crowd against him, threatening him, commanding him to speak.

Braceway was amazed by the intensity of Bristow's glance, the tautness of his body, the harsh authority in his voice. This man who had been ill a few hours before exhibited now a strength and a vitality that would have been remarkable in anybody. In him, under the circumstances, it was nothing short of marvellous.

Morley could not withstand him.

"I don't know anything—anything worth while," he said weakly, trembling from head to foot. "I would have told it at the very—at the very first; only I thought it might keep me in Furmville too long. I wanted to get back here and——"

"Never mind about what you wanted!" Bristow's hand fell and gripped his shoulder painfully, shook him, brought him back to the main issue. "What did you see? That's what we want to know, every bit of it, all of it!"

Morley flinched, trying to throw off Bristow's hand. The lame man stepped back.

"All right," he said, "I'm not going to hurt you."

Morley, having yielded, told his story hurriedly, with little pauses here and there, struggling for breath.

"I did miss my train, the midnight," he began. "I really tried to catch it. But, when I found it was gone, I couldn't sleep. I was worried and frightened. This bank business was on my mind. I wanted to think." He forced a mirthless smile at that. "I couldn't think very straight, but I tried to. I couldn't do anything but see myself in jail, in the penitentiary, because of the bank.

"I wandered around without paying any attention to where I was. I'd left my bags in the station. The first thing I knew, I was on Manniston Road, in front of Number Nine—your house. I felt tired, and I sat down on the bottom step. I had on a raincoat. It—it was pitch-dark there.

"The two electric lights, the street lights, on that block were out—had burnt out, or something. The only light I could see was down at the corner, where Manniston Road goes into Freeman Avenue —and that didn't give any light where I was."

"That's true," Bristow said sharply, "but, from where you sat, anybody going up or down the steps of Number Five would have been directly between you and the avenue light. Isn't that so?"

"Yes."

"All right—go ahead. What did you see?"

Morley hitched back his chair still further. He had begun to perspire, and he kept running his fingers round his neck between flesh and collar.

"It was raining," he went on, his voice strained and metallic, "a fine drizzle at that time, and this made a circle of light, a kind of bright screen around the avenue light. Things that happened on, or near, the steps of Number Five were silhouetted against that screen of light.

"I'd been there just a little while when I noticed some kind of movement on the steps of Number Five. It was a man coming down the steps. He was very careful about it, and very slow; looked like a man on his tiptoes."

Bristow maintained his attitude of hanging over him, urging him on, forcing him to talk. Braceway and Major Ross, their faces wearing strained expressions, bent forward in their chairs, catching every syllable that came from the prisoner.

"He went down the steps and turned down Manniston Road, toward the avenue."

"All right!" Bristow prompted. "What then?"

"That was all there was to that. I just sat there. It looked funny to me, but I didn't follow him. I wondered what he'd been doing. I never thought about murder or—or anything like that. I swear I didn't!"

He licked his lips and gulped.

"I sat there, I don't know how much longer it was—pretty long, I suppose. I didn't keep my glance always toward Number Five.

"When I did look that way again, I saw another man come down the steps quietly, very cautiously. He turned toward me, but he came only far enough up to cut in between Number Five and Number Seven. He disappeared that way, between the two houses."

"Did you see the struggle?" Braceway asked sharply.

Bristow scowled at the interruption.

"What struggle?" Morley retorted, vacant eyes turned toward Braceway.

"You know! The struggle between two men at the foot of the steps of Number Five."

"I didn't see a struggle," said Morley. "There wasn't any."

"You might as well tell it straight now as later. Give me the truth about that struggle. Were you in it?"

"No."

"Now, see here! We know such a struggle occurred. If you were there, as you say you were, you must have seen it. You couldn't have helped seeing it!"

Morley denied it again, and his denial stood against all of Braceway's skill. There had been no struggle, no encounter of any two persons. He clung to that without qualification.

Bristow knew how great Braceway's disappointment was. He was convinced that Braceway, in coming to Washington, had looked forward to securing a confirmation of Withers' story. Now, instead of corroboration, he got only a flat and unshaken contradiction.

CHAPTER XXIII

ON THE RACK

BRACEWAY waved his hand carelessly, relinquishing the post of questioner. Bristow took command again.

"What did you do after you saw the second man?"

"At first, I sat still. After a while, not very long, it occurred to me that the two women in Number Five might be in danger. I say it occurred to me, but I didn't really think so.

"I walked down to the bungalow, but I couldn't hear any noise, couldn't see any light. Finally, I went up to the head of the steps and listened, but there wasn't a sound. Then I went back to the hotel—no; I went first to the station, got my grips, and then went to the hotel."

"Didn't murder or robbery occur to you when you saw those two men on the steps?"

"Well—no; I can't say either occurred to me."

"What did, then?"

"I knew Withers had visited his wife unexpectedly once or twice before, late at night."

"Why?"

"I don't know. I thought he was jealous, suspicious."

"And you also thought these two men you saw were Withers?"

"They might have been one man, the same man,"

Morley advanced the supposition wearily. The tremor of his hands had gone into his arms; they jerked every few moments. "I saw them at different times.

"I couldn't see that clearly. But—but I think the first one wore a long raincoat, or else he was heavily built. Hearing about the negro the next day, I thought the first figure I'd seen must have been the negro's. The second didn't look very different. He might have had a beard; perhaps, he was a little slenderer. Those are the only differences I remember."

"Did the second wear a raincoat?"

"I thought so."

"And the first had no beard?"

"He might have, but I don't think so."

Bristow paused long enough to let the silence become impressive. Then he broke the stillness with a voice that cracked sharp as a revolver shot.

"Well! What about the struggle at the foot of the steps?"

Morley, startled by the unexpected abruptness, answered shakily.

"I tell you I—I didn't see any struggle. That man, or those men, tried not to make any noise at all. He thought nobody saw him."

Braceway took a hand again in the examination, but their combined efforts got nothing further from the tired prisoner.

They tried to shake him with the accusation that he had entered the bungalow Monday night; they told him also they might take him back to Furmville at once, charged with the murder.

"It wouldn't make any difference to me," he said, making a weak attempt to laugh. "It wouldn't matter now. I'm not anxious to live anyhow."

Without warning, utter collapse struck him. He flung himself half-around on his chair so that his arms rested on its back, cradling his face. His body was contorted by gasping sobs, and his feet tapped the floor with the rapidity of those of a man running at top speed.

They left him with Major Ross. On the way back to the hotel, Bristow asked:

"What about Withers' story of his struggle—the 'big, strong man' who flung him down the walk?"

"There must have been another, a third man who came down the steps," Braceway answered quietly.

"An assumption," observed Bristow, "which rather strains my credulity."

Braceway said nothing.

"I believe," Bristow spoke up again, "what the fellow said tonight was true—substantially true."

"Do you?" retorted Braceway, thoroughly noncommittal.

"Anyway there remains the problem of who pawned the Withers emeralds and diamonds this afternoon."

"It may not be a problem," said Braceway. "It may be that they weren't the Withers stuff at all."

"Ah! I hadn't thought of that."

They entered the hotel and sat down in the lobby, now almost deserted.

"I think," Bristow announced, careful to keep any note of triumph out of his voice, "I'll go back to Furmville in the morning." He yawned and stretched himself. "I'm about all in, weak as a kitten. What are you planning?"

Braceway's chin was thrust forward. He looked belligerent, angry.

"I'm going to Baltimore tomorrow. I intend to run down every clue I have or can find. I'm going to take up every statement he made tonight and dissect it—every point. I want all the facts—all of them."

Bristow turned so as to face him squarely.

"Why don't you go back with me? Why keep on fighting what I've proved? I think I know why you came to Washington. It wasn't your belief in Morley's guilt. It was your desire to clear Withers. But you know as well as I do that Withers isn't guilty. So, why worry?"

Braceway sprang to his feet.

"Morley isn't out of the woods yet," he said grimly. "This case isn't settled yet, by a long shot. I'm going to stick right here."

He made no reference to Withers.

Bristow went to his room, paid and dismissed Miss Martin, and began to undress. He was more than satisfied with everything that had happened. He had bested Braceway again, this time finally; his reputation as a "consulting detective" was more than safe; and, knowing now why Braceway had pursued Morley, he would return to Furmville in the morning, his mind thoroughly at ease.

CHAPTER XXIV

MISS FULTON WRITES A LETTER

AS long as the public's morbid curiosity clamoured for details of the case, the newspapers provided them lavishly. This curiosity was intensified by two things: first, the search for a murderer after so much almost convincing evidence had been found against the negro, and, second, the duel between Bristow, the amateur, and Braceway, the professional, each bent on making his theory "stand up." The amateur had achieved far more celebrity than he had expected.

It would have been hard to find two men less alike than he and Braceway. Bristow was capable now and then of manifesting the strength and impressive authority he had exhibited in his questioning of Morley. Braceway, on the other hand, was always keyed up, dashing, imperious. And he had a kindness of heart, a very live tenderness, such as the lame man never displayed.

Braceway was of the tribe of dreamers.

He had learned that no man may hope to be a great detective unless he has imagination, unless he can throw into the dark places which always surround a mysterious crime the luminous and golden glow of fancy. He had found also that, if a man's vocabulary is without a "perhaps" or a "but why couldn't it be the other way?" he will never be able to judge human nature or to consider fairly every side of any question.

He discussed these views at breakfast with Bristow, who was interested only in his own decision of the night before to return at once to Furmville.

"My health demands it," he said; "and I can't convince myself that either you or I can dig up anything here to affect the final outcome of the case."

"You're right about the health part of it; I'm not sure about the other," said Braceway.

"What are you after, though?" Bristow pressed him.

"Facts. That bearded man with the gold tooth, the fellow who always started from nowhere and invariably vanished into thin air—I don't propose to assume that he had nothing to do with the murder of Enid Withers. I don't intend to be recorded as not having combed the country for him if necessary.

"That disguised man is no myth. And Morley knows all about beard 'make-up.' His note to me in Furmville proved that. The negro boy, Roddy, swears Morley and the mysterious stranger are the same.

"There isn't a crook living who can put it over on me this way with a cheap disguise. And this case isn't cleared up until, in some way, I find out who he is or get my hands on him." His voice was vibrant with the intensity of his feeling. "I'm going to find him! I intend to answer, to my own satisfaction, two questions."

"What are they?"

"The first is: was the bearded man Morley? The second: if Morley wasn't the bearded man, who was?"

"But, if you do find this hirsute individual, what then? What becomes of the unassailable evidence against the negro?"

"That will come later. Today I'm going to Baltimore. I've a report already, this morning, from Platt. He went over there last night. Morley, I find, deceived us again last night. He said nothing of leaving the hotel to call on the lawyer, Taliaferro.

"As a matter of fact, he did visit Taliaferro.

"He called the lawyer on the telephone at twenty minutes past two and said he would go at once to his office. If he had done so, he would have arrived there at twenty-four minutes past two. He reached there, in fact, at two-fifty, ten minutes of three. A half-hour of his time isn't accounted for. He left the hotel at two-twenty-one. Where did he spend that last half-hour? It's an interesting point."

"Yes," Bristow said, surprised. "Pawnshops?"

"Perhaps—two pawnshops."

"And the pawned diamonds and emeralds are certainly the Withers stuff, a part of it?"

"I'm sure of it."

"Anyway you look at it," Bristow smiled pleasantly, his manner tinged with patronizing. "you've a hard job to get away with."

"If," the other ruminated, "the jewels pawned

yesterday were not Mrs. Withers', why wouldn't the man who pawned them come forward and say so? If there wasn't anything crooked about them, why should he hide himself? The papers are full of it this morning. It's public property."

Bristow, looking at his watch, saw that it was nine o'clock and time for him to go to the railroad station.

They said good-bye, each confident that the other was on the wrong trail.

"I'm leaving you," the lame man declared, "to run to your heart's content around the clever circles you've outlined, and to beat off the newspaper reporters."

"It's not for long," Braceway returned seriously. "I hope to be in Furmville next week with an armful of new facts. I'll see you then."

He went to the desk and got his mail. In addition to reports from his Atlanta office, there was one letter in a big, square envelope. He recognized the writing and opened that first.

"Dear Mr. Braceway," it said: "I hope Mr. Bristow repeated to you everything I told him. He is quite brilliant, I have no doubt, but I talked to him in the belief and hope that he would tell you everything. I know what you can do, and I trust you more than I do him. You see, you have successes behind you.

"If he did not tell you all, I shall be glad to do so at any time."

It was signed, "Sincerely yours, Maria Fulton."

He read the note twice. When he put it into his pocket, there was a new light in his eyes, and at the corners of his mouth a relaxation of the lines of sternness.

"I wonder——" he began in his thoughts, and added: "Some other time, perhaps. No; surely. I always knew her better than she knew herself."

He was frankly happy, felt himself uplifted, freshened in spirit. Standing there in the crowded lobby, with people brushing past him and jogging his elbow, he flashed back two years in memory to the evening when he had warned her not to let the sweetness of her personality be overshadowed by her sister. It was then that he had insisted on her living her own life instead of giving up to the wishes of others always.

She had misconstrued it, deciding that he was disappointed in her. She said his love for her had lessened, and therefore their engagement was a great mistake.

Then came her promise to marry Morley, a promise made in pique. Afterwards she had done everything possible to show the world she had chosen a man instead of a weakling. This, Braceway knew, was why she had advanced him money, bolstering up one mistake with another. It was why she had listened to his stories of getting great wealth, if only he had a small amount of money to start on!

What a fiasco the whole thing had been, what bitter disappointment and sorrow! And yet, she had been fortunate in discovering now what he was.

There was no doubt about it, Braceway decided; she had loved him, Braceway, all this time. In a few days he would tell her so, make her confess it. He would compel her to listen to what he had to say; he would never again jeopardize their happiness by allowing her to misunderstand him.

He crossed the lobby with long, springy strides. He felt that he could encounter no obstacle too great for him to overcome. Failure could not touch him.

He left the hotel and went to Golson's office. He had much to do in Baltimore—and elsewhere.

Hurrying to the station after a brief conference with Golson, he wondered why he had heard nothing from Withers. What was the matter with George anyhow? Why hadn't he acknowledged the telegram of yesterday? Couldn't he realize, without being told, that he might be charged with the murder at any moment?

Braceway was as well aware as Bristow of the rising flood of criticism against Withers.

"If I can't bring things to a last show-down within a day or two," he looked the situation squarely in the face, "it will be uncomfortable for him—emphatically uncomfortable."

He turned to a study of the questions he wanted to put to Eidstein, this kindly old merchant who was so considerate, so handsomely considerate, about buying back jewels he had once sold. Mr. Eidstein, he felt sure, must be an interesting character.

CHAPTER XXV

A MYSTIFYING TELEGRAM

REACHING Furmville early Sunday morning, Bristow went straight to his bungalow, where Mattie had breakfast waiting for him.

"You is sholy some big man now, Mistuh Bristow!" she informed him. "Sence you been gawn, folks done made it a habit to drive by hyuh jes' foh de chanct uv seein' you."

Before the day was over, he found that this was true. And he liked it. He spent a great deal of his time on the front porch, finding it far from unpleasant to be regarded as a second Sherlock Holmes.

Late in the afternoon his Cincinnati friend, Overton, called on him, puffing and gasping for breath as he climbed the steps. Bristow was glad to see him; it afforded him an opportunity to discuss his success. He did not try to delude himself in that regard; he was proud of what he had accomplished—rightfully proud, he told himself—and pleased with his plans for the future.

"Gee whiz!" the fat man panted. "This hill is something fierce. It's only your sudden dash into the limelight that drags me up here."

"You behold"—Bristow softened his statement

with a deprecating laugh—"Mr. Lawrence Bristow, a finished, honest-to-heaven detective, a criminologist."

"What do you mean?"

"I'm going to make it my profession. I'm starting out as a professional detective."

Overton burst into bubbling laughter.

"That's rich!" he exclaimed. "You'd never in the world make good at it. Why, Bristow, you're lame; you've a crooked nose; that heavy, overhanging lip of yours—those things would enable any crook to spot you a mile off." He laughed again. "I'd like to see you shadowing some foxy second-story worker!"

"I said 'a consulting detective'," Bristow corrected him. "That shadowing business is for the hired man, the square-toed, bull-necked cops. I'll work only as the directing head, the brains of the investigations."

"Oh, that's different," said Overton, at once conciliatory. "That's nearer real sense. Big money in it, isn't there?"

"Yes. I'm not an eleemosynary institution yet."

Overton mopped his fat cheeks.

"Ah, me!" he sighed. "We never know what's ahead of us, do we? A year ago you were dubbing around in Cincinnati trying to sell real estate and working out crime problems on paper—and here you are now, a big man. It's hard to believe."

"It is, however, a very acceptable fact."

"No doubt, no doubt," assented the fat man.

On Overton's heels came the chief of police. After getting a minute recital of what had happened in Washington and Baltimore, he agreed that Braceway was only setting up straw men for the pleasure of knocking them down.

"Even if there is something mysterious in Morley's conduct, in what occurred in Baltimore," said the chief, "it can't do away with the open-and-shut fact that Perry did the murder."

"Of course," Bristow commented. "But what's the news with you?"

"For one thing, Perry gave us last night what he calls a confession. In it he says he did tell Lucy Thomas he knew where he could get money 'or something just as good'; he did go to Number Five in a more or less drunken condition; and he got as far as the front door.

"There, he says, he thought he heard a noise across the road from him, and he lost his nerve. He tiptoed down the steps and went away, passing in between Number Five and Number Seven. He ran all the way back to Lucy's house, threw down the key he had got from her, and then went to his own rooming-house. He says he stayed there the rest of the night."

"Is that all?"

"That's all."

"How about the lavalliere? Wasn't it found under his window? The papers said so."

"Yes; in the grass in the yard. But he denies knowing anything about it."

"Of course! And his confession is nothing but a confirmation of the case against him."

"Exactly. He seems to want to hang himself. And he'll do it. The grand jury meets next Thursday. He'll be indicted then, and tried two weeks later."

"What are the people here saying about Braceway's bitterness against Morley? Anything?"

"Yes. I'd meant to tell you about that. Some of the gossip hits Withers pretty hard. They can't understand what's behind this persecution of Morley after it's been proved that Perry did the murder. You've seen hints of it in the papers.

"And it looks queer. Some say Withers is guilty, out-and-out guilty, and afraid the case against Perry won't hold good. So, they say, he wants to get a case against Morley."

"A sort of second line of defense?"

"I reckon so. But, then, there are others saying right now that Morley was mixed up in some sort of scandal for which Withers wants revenge. That's what you said at the very start. Remember?"

Bristow laughed softly.

"Yes; I had that idea, and I've reasoned it out. On the way to Washington, and after we got there, I saw that Braceway wasn't entirely frank with me. You know how a man can feel a thing like that. He gets it by intuition.

"And it worried me. Having handled the case here, I didn't want him to spring some brand new angle which possibly, in some way, might make me look like a fool.

"I puzzled over the thing a whole lot. What was it he was after without letting me in on it? The night we talked to Morley in the station house, I got it. We were in a cab at the time, a lucky thing, because, when it burst upon me, I narrowly escaped hysterics. The thing came to me like an inspiration.

"Braceway was afraid Morley knew something detrimental to Withers and would spring it under questioning. Understand now: it wasn't directly connected with the murder, but something that would make it pretty hot for Withers. And here was the laugh: while Morley didn't know it, I did. Braceway had made the trip to gag Morley, to see that he didn't uncover something which, after all, Morley didn't know—and I did!

"It was this: about nine months ago Mrs. Withers, while in Washington, got a lawyer, the firm of Dutton & Dutton, to draw up for her the necessary papers for suing Withers for a divorce. In these documents she set forth in so many words that her husband had treated her with the utmost brutality, so much so that she lived daily in danger of death while under his roof.

"She regarded him, she swore, as capable of murdering her at any time. Now, do you see? If that had gotten into the newspapers, if Morley had known of it through Maria Fulton and had blurted it out, no power on earth could have kept down the very reasonable assumption that Withers had had a hand in his wife's death—or, at least, had regarded it with complaisance.

"No wonder I laughed, was it? But I said nothing about it to Braceway. I couldn't have explained to him how I knew it, although the tip came to me straight enough. And, as there's no earthly chance of Withers having been implicated in the crime, why worry about it?

"I merely laughed and—kept quiet."

Greenleaf had listened in great solemnity to this amusing recital.

"Maybe you're right," he said. "But Withers has done some funny things."

"What things?"

"His wife was buried in Atlanta Thursday morning. He immediately left Atlanta, and hasn't been seen or heard of since—a sharp contrast to old Fulton. He got back here early Friday morning and came up to Number Five. They're going to keep that bungalow."

"When did Withers leave Atlanta?"

"Thursday morning, right after the funeral. Another thing: he's heels over head in debt."

"Well, what about it? What are you driving at?" Bristow asked, perceptibly irritable.

"I'm not driving at anything. What's it to us anyway? It stimulates this ugly talk. That's all."

Bristow was doing some quick thinking. If Withers had left Atlanta early Thursday morning, he might have reached Washington by Friday afternoon—and gone to Baltimore! But did he? And did Braceway know of it and keep it to himself?

He recalled that Braceway, during their breakfast together in Washington, had said:

"Get one thing straight in your mind, Bristow. Any man I find mixed up in this murder I'm going to turn over to the police. If I thought George Withers had killed his wife, I'd hand him over so fast it would make your head swim. You may not believe that, but I would—in a second!"

Had that been a prophecy? Was Withers in Baltimore at two-thirty Friday afternoon? Could he have been fool enough to pawn anything? Or did he go there in the hope of incriminating Morley further? All these things were within the realm of possibility, but hardly credible. Braceway might have known of them, and he might not.

Abrahamson, he remembered, had put it into Braceway's head, against Braceway's own desire, that the man with the gold tooth and Withers resembled each other. But nobody believed that. It would be futile to consider it.

The chief, as if reading his thoughts, gave more information:

"Abrahamson, the loan-shark, came to my office yesterday; wanted to know where he could reach Braceway by wire. He evidently knew something and wouldn't tell me. Said he wired yesterday morning to Braceway in Washington, but the telegraph company reported 'no delivery'—couldn't locate him. I wonder what the Jew knows."

"It's too much for me." Bristow dismissed the question carelessly, but immediately flared up peevishly: "What's getting into these fellows? They act like fools, each of them, Morley and Withers, following Perry's lead and trying to have themselves arrested! But Braceway—if he wasn't in Washington, he must be on his way back here. We'll soon have his last say on the case."

"All the same," said Greenleaf, "if I were in that husband's place, I'd stay away from here. The talk's too bitter; worse here among the Manniston Road people than anywhere else."

"Well, what of it?"

"It wouldn't be the first instance of how easy it is for an innocent man to be—well, hurt."

"Oh, that sort of thing is out of the question, absurd."

"Never mind! I'd stay away. That's what I'd do."

It was almost dark when the chief of police took his departure. Bristow sat watching the last crimson light fade over the mountains. The dim electric, a poor excuse for a street lamp, had flashed on in front of No. 4. The shadows grew deeper and deeper; there was no breeze; the oaks along the roadside and in the backyards became still, black plumes above the bungalows.

Manniston Road was wrapped in darkness. The silence was broken, even at this early hour, only by the distant, faint screech of street-car wheels against the rails, or the far sound of an automobile horn down in the town, or the rattle of a sick man's cough on one of the sleeping porches. There was something uncanny, Bristow thought, in the velvet blackness and the heavy silence.

He got up and went into the living room, turning on the lights. The night, the stillness, had affected him. Perhaps, he thought, Withers after all would do well to give Furmville a wide berth. If disorganized rumour grew into positive accusation——

And what of himself, Bristow? He had run down the guilty man, had discovered and hooked together the facts that made retribution almost an accomplished thing. Could he have been mistaken, entirely wrong? Would public opinion turn also against him and say he had enmeshed an innocent negro instead of bringing to punishment a jealousy-maddened husband?

Was there a chance that, in condemning Withers, they would destroy his reputation for brilliant work?

Pshaw! He shrugged his shoulders. He was worse than the gossiping women, letting himself conjure up weird and incredible ideas. There was not a weak place, not an illogical point, in the case he had disclosed against Carpenter. He had won. His prestige was assured. Far from questioning his work, they ought to thank him for——

The reverie was interrupted by the telephone bell. He took down the receiver and shouted "Hello!" as if he resented the call. His irritation showed what a tremendous amount of nervous energy he had expended in the last six days.

"Western Union speaking," said a man's voice. "Telegram for Mr. Lawrence Bristow, nine Manniston Road."

"All right. This is Bristow. Read it to me."

"Message is dated today, Washington, D. C.—'Mr. Lawrence Bristow, nine Manniston Road, Furmville, N. C. See Encyclopaedia Britannica, volume one, page five hundred and six, second column, line fifteen to line seventeen, and page five hundred and seven, second column, line seventeen to line twenty-three.' Signed 'S. S. Braceway.' Do you get that?"

"No! Wait a minute," he called out sharply. "Let me get a pencil and take it down."

He did so, verifying the numbers by having the operator repeat the message a third time. When he had hung up the receiver, he sat staring at what he had written. It was like so much Greek to him.

"What's it all about?" he puzzled. "Is it one of Braceway's jokes?"

Then he remembered that Braceway was not that kind of a joker. He looked at his watch. He had no encyclopaedia, and it was now a quarter to eleven, too late to ring up anybody and ask the absurd favour of having extracts from an encyclopaedia read to him over the telephone. Besides, it might be something he would prefer to keep to himself.

He would wait until morning and go to the public library where he could look up the references with no questions asked. He was annoyed by the necessity of delay, angry with Braceway. He studied the numbers again, and allowed himself the rare luxury of an outburst of vari-coloured profanity.

The idea uppermost in his mind was that the telegram had to do with Withers—or could it be something about Morley?

In his bed on the sleeping porch, he looked out at the black plumes of the trees. The silence seemed now neither sinister nor oppressive. All that was sinister was in the past; had ended the night of the murder; and Carpenter would go to the chair for it—sure.

And yet, if he were Withers, he would not come back to Manniston Road. Nobody could foresee what Braceway might imagine and exaggerate, even if it indicted and condemned his closest friend.

CHAPTER XXVI

WANTED: VENGEANCE

BUT the next morning was the crowded beginning of the biggest day in Bristow's life, and the trip to the library was delayed. The hired automobile was waiting in front of No. 9 when a second telegram came, a bulky dispatch, scrawled with a pen across several pages.

Dated from New Orleans, it read:

"Reward of five thousand dollars for discovery of my seven-year-old son within next six days. Kidnapped last Friday night. No clue so far. Am most anxious for your help. Will pay you two thousand dollars and expenses and in addition to that will pay you the reward money if you are successful. Will pay the two thousand whether you succeed or not. City and state authorities will give you all the help needed. Come at once if possible. Wire answer.

(Signed) "Emile Loutois."

It was characteristic of Bristow that he was not particularly surprised or elated by the request for his services. It was the kind of thing he had foreseen as a result of the advertising he had received.

He made his decision at once. For the past two

days the Loutois kidnapping had commanded big space in the newspapers, and he was familiar with the story. Emile Loutois, Jr., young son of the wealthiest sugar planter in Louisiana, had been spirited away from the pavement in front of his home. It had been done at twilight with striking boldness, and no dependable trace of the kidnappers had been found.

The delivery boy was waiting on the porch. Bristow typewrote his reply on a sheet of note paper:

"Terms accepted. Starting for New Orleans at once."

On his way to the door, he stopped and reflected. He went back to the typewriter and sat down. He had not yet found out the real meaning of the Braceway message; and he did not propose to leave Furmville until he was assured that nothing could be done to blur the brightness of his work on the Withers case.

He realized, and at the same time resented, the tribute he paid Braceway through his hesitancy. The man was a clever detective and, if left to dominate Greenleaf unopposed, might easily focus attention on a new theory of the crime. Not that this could result in the acquittal of the negro; but it might deprive him, Bristow, of the credit he was now given.

Wouldn't it be well for him to stay in Furmville another twenty-four hours? There was Fulton; he wanted to learn how fully he approved of Braceway's refusal to accept the case against Perry,

Carpenter. Moreover, it seemed essential now that he discover the whereabouts of Withers. And twenty-four hours could hardly change anything in the kidnapping case.

He tore up what he had written, and rattled off:

"Held here twenty-four hours longer by Withers case. Start to New Orleans tomorrow morning. Terms accepted."

As he handed it to the boy, he saw Mr. Fulton coming up the steps. He greeted the old gentleman with easy, smiling cordiality and pushed forward a chair for him, giving no sign of impatience at being delayed in his trip to the library.

The simple dignity and strength of Fulton's bearing was even more impressive than it had been during their first talk. The lines were still deep in his face, but his eyes glowed splendidly, and this time, when he rested his hands on the chair-arms, they were steady.

"I've come to beg news," he announced, his apologetic smile very winning.

"Just what news?" returned Bristow. "I'll be glad to give you anything I can."

"The real results of your trip; that's what I'd like to know about. I got no letter or telegram from Sam Braceway this morning; no report at all."

Bristow told him the story in generous detail, concluding with his conviction that Morley, although a thorough scoundrel, was innocent of any hand in the murder.

"I wish I could agree with you," said the old man. "I wish we all could satisfy our minds and take the evidence against the negro as final. But we can't. At least, I can't. I can't believe anything but that the disguised man, the one with the beard, is the one we've got to find."

"You still think that man is Morley?"

"I do—which reminds me. I came up here to tell you something I got from Maria, my daughter. She told me she had talked with you quite frankly. Well, she recalls that once she and this Morley were discussing the wearing of beards and moustaches; and he made this remark: 'One thing about a beard, it's the best disguise possible.'"

"That is interesting, Mr. Fulton. Anything else?"

"Yes. He had a good deal to say to that general effect. He said even a moustache, cleverly worn, changed a man's whole expression. That struck me at once, remembering that the jewels were pawned in Baltimore by a man who wore a moustache. Then, too, Morley said something about the value of eyebrows in a disguise, substituting bushy ones for thin ones, or vice versa. He had the whole business at his tongue's end."

"He said all that, in what connection—crime?"

"She can't recall that. She merely remembers he said it. I thought you'd like to know of it."

"Of course. We can't have too many facts. By the way, sir, can you tell me where Mr. Withers is?"

"In Atlanta."

Seeing that he knew nothing of his son-in-law's disappearance, Bristow dropped the subject, and asked:

"What is Miss Fulton's belief now? She still thinks Morley is the man?"

The old man hitched his chair closer to Bristow's and lowered his voice.

"She says a curious thing, Mr. Bristow. She declares that, if Morley isn't guilty, George Withers is."

"And you?"

"Oh, the talk about George is absurd."

"But," urged Bristow, his smile persuasive, "for the sake of argument, if circumstances pointed to him as——"

"I'd spend every dollar I have, use the last atom of my strength, to send him to the chair! No suffering, no torture, would be too much for him—if that's what you mean to ask me. If I even suspected him, I'd subject him to an inquiry more relentless, more searching, more merciless than I'd use with anybody else!"

His nostrils expanded curiously. His eyes flamed.

"Mr. Bristow," he continued, menace in his low tone, "no punishment ever devised by man could be sufficient to pay for, to atone for, the horror, the enormity, of the destruction of such a woman as my daughter was. Mercy? I'd show him no mercy if he lived a thousand years!"

"I understand your feeling," Bristow said. "You're perfectly right, of course. And what I was leading up to is this: although we know that the idea of Withers' guilt is absurd, he's being made to suffer. You've seen intimations, almost direct statements, in the newspapers. People are talking disagreeably.

"They're saying that Braceway, employed by you and Withers, is persecuting this bank thief in the hope of building up the murder charge, so that, if the case against Carpenter falls down, Morley will be the logical man to be put on trial. You see?"

"No," Fulton said; "I don't. What do you mean?"

"That you, Withers, and Braceway are afraid Withers may be accused of the murder."

"Ah! They're saying that, are they? And you were going to say—what?"

"Simply this: the negro's the guilty man. The facts speak for themselves, and facts are incontrovertible. As surely as the sun shines, Carpenter killed your daughter. Why, then, continue this gossip, slander which besmirches Withers and is bound to attack your daughter's name?"

"What do you mean? Be a little more specific, please."

"I mean: what do you and Withers gain by letting Braceway keep this thing before the public?"

Fulton leaned far forward in his chair, his lower lip thrust out, his eyes blazing.

"No, sir!" he exploded. "I'll never call Braceway off! They're gossiping, are they? They can gossip until they're blue in the face. What do I care for public opinion, for gossip, for their leers and whispers? Nothing—not a snap of the finger! To hell with what they say! What I want is vengeance. I'll have it! Call Braceway off? Not while there's breath in me!

He paused and bit on his lip.

"Understand me, Mr. Bristow," he continued, his tone more moderate. "I meant no criticism of you; I know how faithfully you've worked. I realize even that you have proved your case. But I can't accept it, that's all. You'll forgive an old man's temper."

Bristow carried the argument no further. He saw that Fulton, and Withers too, would follow Braceway's lead. Consequently, he was confronted with the necessity of keeping up the idiotic duel with the Atlanta detective.

Moreover, he sensed the viewpoint of the dead woman's family. They were averse to believing she had been the victim of an ordinary negro burglar. Remembering her beauty and charm, her cleverness and lovable qualities, they preferred to think that some one under great emotion, or with a terrific gift for crime, had cut short her brilliant existence.

People, he meditated, find foolish and bizarre means of comforting themselves when overwhelmed by great tragedy. Very well, then; let it go at that. After all, it was not his funeral.

Accompanying Fulton to the sidewalk, he climbed into the automobile and, in a few minutes, was in the library asking for the first volume of the last edition of the Encyclopaedia Britannica. His limp proclaimed his identity, and the young woman at the desk, recognizing him, got the book for him with surprising promptness.

His habits of thought were such that he had not wasted energy during the morning in idle speculation as to what he would find. In fact, he attached but little importance to Braceway's message. He had dismissed it the night before as a queer dodge on the other's part to bolster up his view of the case.

He went to a desk in a remote part of the reading room. Under any circumstances, he would not have cared for the intense and interested scrutiny with which the girl at the desk favoured him. The attitude he took gave her ample opportunity for a study of the back of his head.

Opening the volume, he turned to the first reference, page 506, column 2, line 15 to line 17. At the first word he drew a quick breath; it was sharp enough to sound like a low whistle. He read:

"ALBINO, a biological term (Lat. *albus,* white), in the usual acceptation, for a pigmentless individual of a normally pigmented race."

Putting his finger on the top of the second column, page 507, he counted down to line 17, and read:

"Albinism occurs in all races of mankind, among mountainous as well as lowland dwellers. And, with man, as with other animals, it may be complete or partial. Instances of the latter condition are very common among the negroes of the United States and of South America, and in them assumes a piebald character, irregular white patches being scattered over the general black surface of the body."

Before he began to think, he read the passages carefully a second time. Then he continued to hold the book open, staring at it as if he still read.

The importance of the words struck him immediately. He grasped their meaning as quickly and as fully as he would have done if Braceway had stood beside him and explained. The skin of a white person and that of an albino show up the same under a microscope: white. If a man had under his finger nails particles of white skin, he could have collected them there by scratching an albino as well as by scratching a Caucasian, a white woman.

And Lucy Thomas was an albino. He was certain of that; did not question it for a moment. Braceway had assured himself of that before sending the telegram.

Perry Carpenter had had a fight or a tussle with her in securing the key to No. 5 the night of the murder, and in the scoffling he had scratched her. That, at least, would be Perry's story and Lucy's. Braceway had been certain of that also before wiring to him.

As a matter of fact, Braceway had known all this before they had started for Washington and had kept it back, playing with him, laughing up his sleeve. The thought nettled him, finally made him thoroughly angry. He compelled himself to weigh the new situation carefully.

Well, what of it, even if Lucy were an albino and Perry had scratched her? Did that affect materially the case against Perry? There was still evidence to prove that he had been to the Withers' bungalow. He had confessed it himself. And the lavalliere incidents and the blouse buttons substantiated it still further.

The albino argument was by no means final, could not be made definite. The fact remained that there had been scratches on the murdered woman's hand and that particles of a white person's skin had been found under Perry's finger nails. That was not to be denied. Of course, the negro's attorney could argue that these particles had come from Lucy Thomas, not from Mrs. Withers.

But it would be only an argument. The jury would pass judgment on it—and he was willing to leave it to the jury.

He closed the book, took it back to the desk and thanked the young woman. There was nothing in his appearance to indicate disappointment. In fact, he felt none. By the time he reached home he had gone over the whole thing once more and dismissed it as of no real consequence. Braceway's discovery, or his making the discovery known, had come too late.

If it had been brought out ahead of Perry's confession—yes; it would have made quite a difference then.

"Let the heathen rage!" he thought, remembering the bitter stubbornness with which Braceway and Fulton denied the negro's guilt.

Braceway's withholding the albino information, playing him for a fool, recurred to him, and the accustomed flush on his cheeks grew deeper. He would not forget that; he would pay it back—with interest.

He turned to the Loutois case. Going to his typewriter, he made a list of New Orleans, Atlanta, and New York newspapers.

"Mattie," he called, "I want you to go down to a news-stand, the big one; I think it's at the corner of Haywood and Patton."

He handed her money.

"And here's a list of the papers you're to get. Ask for all of them published since last Friday. Be as quick as you can. I'm in a hurry."

When she came back, she brought also the early edition of the Furmville afternoon paper. He glanced at it, looking for Washington or Baltimore news of Braceway's activities. He found it on the front page. The headlines read:

FINDS NEW EVIDENCE
ON WITHERS MURDER

MORLEY GUILTY, OR—WHO?

Whereabouts of Murdered Woman's Husband
Not Known—Braceway Predicts New
and Amazing Disclosure.

The dispatch itself was:

"Washington, D. C., May 14.—That an entirely

new light will soon be thrown on the brutal murder of Mrs. Enid Fulton Withers, beauty and society favourite of Atlanta and Washington, became known here today.

"Samuel S. Braceway, probably the ablest private detective in this country, left this city yesterday afternoon for Furmville, N. C., the scene of the crime, after he had completed an exhaustive investigation here and in Baltimore of more or less obscure matters related to the murder. Police officials here state that the negro, Perry Carpenter, now held in the Furmville jail for the crime, will never go to trial.

"This, they claim, will be but one result of the work Braceway did here and in Baltimore. The detective himself was reticent when interviewed just before he caught his train, but, as he stood on the platform, nobbily dressed and twirling his walking stick, he was the picture of confidence.

"'I think you're safe in saying,' he admitted 'that the Withers case hasn't yet been settled. We're due for some surprising disclosures unless I miss my guess.'

"'Can you tell us anything about the suspicions directed against Henry Morley?' he was asked.

"'It's Morley or—somebody else,' Braceway said smilingly. 'Anybody can study the facts and satisfy himself on that point.'

"'Who's the somebody else?'

"'We'll know pretty soon. In fact, things should develop in less than a week, considerably less than a week.'

"One of the interesting sidelights on this mysterious murder case, it was learned this morning, is that the whereabouts of the murdered woman's husband, George S. Withers of Atlanta, is at present unknown. Dispatches from Atlanta say he disappeared from there the morning his wife's funeral took place. Advices from Furmville are that he is not there with his father-in-law and sister-in-law. Braceway said yesterday he knew nothing of Withers' whereabouts."

Beneath the Washington dispatch was one from Atlanta:

"Inquiry made here today failed to disclose where George S. Withers, husband of the victim of the brutal crime at Furmville, N. C., is now. He left this city the morning Mrs. Withers was buried, according to his friends, but said nothing as to his destination or the probable length of time he would be away.

"The Atlanta authorities were asked by the Washington police to locate him if possible. No reason for the request was given."

There was a smile on Bristow's lips when he tossed the paper to one side. Braceway, he deduced from the article, was having his troubles making the Morley theory hang together. And why should he hurry back to Furmville? There was nothing new here.

He shrugged his shoulders and unwrapped the bundle of out-of-town papers.

Recalling how late he had received the albino message the night before, he concluded that Braceway had filed it in Washington during the afternoon, with instructions that it be sent as a night message. His resentment for Braceway flared up again.

" 'Amazing disclosure,' " he mentally quoted the headlines. "Well, we shall see what we shall see. Perhaps, it will come as an amazing disclosure to him that I've been on the sound side of this question all along."

He began the work of cutting from the papers the accounts of the Loutois kidnapping. As he read them, he built up a tentative outline showing who the kidnappers were and where they probably had secreted the boy. He grew absorbed, whistling in a low key.

So far as he was concerned, the Withers case was a closed incident.

Early in the afternoon he called Greenleaf on the telephone, and announced:

"I'm leaving town for a few days tomorrow morning."

"Again! What for?" the chief asked.

"They've asked me to work out that kidnapping case in New Orleans—the Loutois child."

"Good! I'm glad to hear it; I congratulate you."

Greenleaf was sincerely pleased. He felt that he had sponsored and developed the lame man as a detective.

"Thanks. Before I go, I want to have a talk with you. We might as well go over everything once more and——"

"That reminds me. I was just about to call you up, but your news made me forget. I've a wire from Braceway, just got it. He filed it at Salisbury, on his way here. Let me read it to you:

"'Have all the stuff I can get on Withers case. Can not go further before conferring with you, Bristow, Fulton, and Abrahamson. Please arrange meeting of all these Bristow's bungalow eight tonight. Withers not with me.'"

"That fits in," Bristow commented; "lets me start for New Orleans on the late night train."

"Wonder what he's got," the chief questioned. "Do you know?"

"No. And I don't believe it amounts to anything. Still, if he wants to talk, we might as well hear it."

"Sure! You can count on me. I'll be there."

"All right," said Bristow. "I'll see you at eight, then."

He went to the sleeping porch and lay down.

"'Withers not with me,'" the last words of the telegram lingered in his mind. "Why did he add that? What's that to do with a conference here tonight?"

Suddenly the answer occurred to him.

"It's Withers!" he thought, at first only half-credulous. "He's going to put it on Withers; he's going to try to put it on Withers."

He paused, thinking "wild" for a moment, so great was his surprise.

"It was Withers he was after from the start,—was it?"

CHAPTER XXVII

THE REVELATION

BRACEWAY and Maria Fulton had upon their faces that expression which announces a happy understanding between lovers. The light of surrender was in her eyes, contented surrender to the man who, because of his love, had asserted his mastery of her. And his voice, as he spoke to her, was all a vibrant tenderness. He realized that he had found and finally made certain his happiness, had done so at the very moment of making public his greatest professional triumph.

For his visit to her he had stolen a half-hour from the rush of work that had devolved upon him since reaching Furmville a few hours ago. He found her as he had expected; she fulfilled his prophecy that, in following her own ideals, she would take her place in the world as a fascinating personality, a lovable woman.

But, while he studied and praised her new charm, he was conscious, more keenly so than ever before, that his success would affect her greatly, would challenge all her strength and courage. And yet, even if it hurt her, it had to be done. It was his duty, and the consequences would have to take care of themselves.

Although, in her turn, she regarded him with the fine intuition of the woman who loves, she got no intimation of his worry. He had determined not to burden her with the details in advance. If what he was about to do should link her dead sister with a pitiless scandal, she would meet it bravely.

Unless he had been confident of that, he could not have loved her. His task was to hand over to justice the guilty man, and not even his concern for the woman he would marry could interfere with his seeing the thing through.

After it was all over, he would come back to comfort her. Their new happiness would counterbalance all. So he thought, with confidence.

A glance through the window showed him Greenleaf and Abrahamson coming slowly up Manniston Road. It was eight o'clock. A few moments later he and Mr. Fulton joined them on the sidewalk. They went at once to No. 9.

Bristow received them in his living room, the table still littered with newspaper clippings on the Loutois kidnapping.

"If the rest of you don't mind," Braceway suggested, "we'd better close the windows. We've a lot of talking to do, and we might as well keep things to ourselves."

The effect of alertness which he always produced was more evident now than ever. He kept his cane and himself in continual motion. While the four other men seated themselves, he remained standing, facing them, his back to the empty fire-place.

"Each of you," he said, "is vitally interested in what I've come here to say. I asked you to have this conference because it affects each of us directly."

His eyes shone, his chin was thrust forward, every ligament in his body was strung taut. And yet, there was nothing of the theatric about him. If he felt excitement, it was suppressed. Determination was the only emotion of which he gave any sign.

"First, however," he supplemented in his light, conversational tone, "how about you?" He indicated with a look Greenleaf and Bristow. "Have you anything new, anything additional?"

With the windows shut, it was noticeably warm and close in the room. Taking off his coat, he tossed it to the chair which had been placed for him. In his white shirt, with dark trousers belted tightly over slender hips, he looked almost boyish.

"No," Bristow answered. "The chief and I went over everything yesterday. We couldn't find a single reason for changing our minds."

"About Carpenter?"

"Yes."

"You mean that's your position, yours and the chief's," Braceway said seriously. "As a matter of fact, the negro's not guilty."

"You mean that's your position," Bristow quoted back to him, his smile indulgent.

"Yes. Carpenter's not guilty, and Morley's not guilty."

Mr. Fulton, who had the chair immediately on the lame man's left, was frankly curious and anxious.

"Before you go any further, Braceway," he interrupted testily, "can you tell us where George Withers is?"

"I can say this much," replied Braceway after a pause: "for reasons best known to himself, Withers refused to join us here. He could have done so if he had wished."

What he said sounded like a direct accusation of Withers. Fulton eyed him incredulously. Bristow took off his coat and settled himself more comfortably in his chair; he was in for a long story, he thought, and, as he had expected last night, the dead woman's husband, not Morley, was to be incriminated.

Greenleaf, lolling back in a rocker near the folding doors of the dining room, gazed at the ceiling, making a show of lack of interest.

Abrahamson, nearest the porch door, was the only auditor thoroughly absorbed in the detective's story and at the same time unreservedly credulous.

"But you know where he is?" Fulton persisted.

"Yes; approximately."

The Jew's sparkling eyes darted from the speaker to the faces of the others. A pleased smile lifted the corners of his mouth toward the great, hooked nose. He anticipated unusually pleasant entertainment.

"But I don't want to waste your time," Braceway continued, taking peculiar care in his choice of words. "When I began work on this case, I thought either the negro or Morley might be the murderer. I changed my mind when I came to think about the mysterious fellow, the man with the brown beard and the gold tooth, the individual who was clever enough to appear and disappear at will, to vanish without leaving a trace so long as he operated at night or in the dusk of early evening.

"I agreed with Mr. Fulton that he was the murderer. Not only that, but he had remarkable ability which he employed for the lowest and most criminal purposes. I first suspected his identity right after my interviews last Wednesday with Roddy, the coloured bellboy, and Mr. Abrahamson, the pawn broker."

"Excuse me," Bristow interposed; "but wasn't it Abrahamson who told you the bearded man looked like Withers?"

Greenleaf grinned, appreciating the lame man's intention to take the wind out of Braceway's sails by giving credit to Abrahamson for the information.

"Yes, he told me that," Braceway answered, as if nettled by the interruption; and added: "Let me finish my statement, Bristow. You can discuss it all you please later on. But I'd prefer to get through with it now.

"Having suspected the identity of the disguised man, I was confronted with two jobs. One was to prove the identity beyond question; the other was to show, by irrefutable evidence, that the disguised man committed the murder. As I said, my theory took shape in my mind that afternoon in my room in the Brevord Hotel. Everything I've done since then, has been for the purpose of getting the necessary facts.

"I have those facts now."

He looked at Greenleaf and Bristow, making it plain that he expected their hostility to anything he had to say.

"My suspicion grew out of my belief that I must find the man who had blackmailed Mrs. Withers in Atlantic City and Washington, and, for the third time, here in Furmville. The blackmailer was the only one who had had access to the victim on the three different occasions of which we know; the work was all by the same hand. Find the blackmailer, and I had the murderer.

"I know now who he is.

"Five years ago there was a striking sort of individuality that had impressed itself on the minds of a good many men in Wall Street, New York City. Although penniless at the outset of his career, and in fact never really rich, he had made a good deal of money now and then; and had spent it as fast as he got it.

"He was brilliant, thoroughly unscrupulous, absolutely without honour. He did the 'Great White Way' stunt—the restaurants, the roof gardens, a pretty actress at times, jewels and champagne. Because of his uncertain habits, he never had an office of his own. He always operated through others. His earning power was a gift of judging the market and knowing when to 'bear' and when to 'bull.'

"This gift was no fabulous thing. It was real in a majority of the times he tried to use it, and because of it he was able to live high and put up a good front. This was the situation up to five years ago. Observe the man's character and the pleasure he took in running crooked.

"With a little study and the usual amount of

industry and concentration, he could have been a power in the financial world. That, however, did not appeal to him. He liked the excitement of crime, the perverted pleasure of playing the crook.

"Early in nineteen-thirteen, a little more than five years ago, the crash came. He was arrested, charged with the embezzlement of thirty-three hundred dollars from the firm which employed him. The name of the firm was Blanchard and Sebastian. He had stolen more than the amount mentioned, but the specific charge on which action was taken was the theft of the thirty-three hundred.

"This man's name was Splain.

"There was a delay of a few hours in arranging for his bail so that he wouldn't have to spend the night in prison. While in his cell, he remarked:

"'This kind of a place doesn't suit me. It's as cold as charity. I'll be out of here in an hour or so, and, if they ever get me into a cell again, they'll have to kill me first. Once is enough.'

"He made good his boast. They didn't get him into one again. He jumped his bail ten days before the date set for his trial. Since then the police have, so far as they know, never laid eyes on him. They had a photograph of him, of course, an adequate description: high aquiline nose; firm, compressed mouth; black and unusually piercing eyes; black hair; all his features sharp-cut; broad shoulders, and slender, athletic figure. Those are some of the details I recall. In——"

Fulton cried out. It was like the shrill, indefinite protest of a child against pain. He put the fingers of his right hand to his forehead, shielding his face. The description of the fugitive had brought instantly to his mind the face of George Withers.

" Indulge me for just a few moments more, Mr. Fulton," Braceway said. " Splain eluded the pursuit. His flight and disappearance were perfectly planned and carried out, and——"

Bristow again interrupted the recital. On his face was a smile which did not reach to his eyes. For the past few minutes he had been thinking faster than he had ever thought in his life, and had made a decision.

" What you've told us," he said calmly, his gaze taking knowledge of no one but the detective, " is, in effect, a rather flattering sketch of a part of my own life."

Greenleaf, with jaw dropped and thinking powers paralyzed, stared at him. Fulton leaned forward as if to spring.

Only Abrahamson, his smile broadening, his cavernous eyes alight, was free from surprise. He had now the air of greatly enjoying the performance he had been invited to see.

Braceway, his shoulders flung back, his figure straight as a poplar, watching Bristow with intense caution, grew suddenly into heroic mould. The red glow from the setting sun streamed through the window to his face, emphasizing the ardour in his eyes. He took a step forward, became dominant, menacing.

His white-clad arm shot out so that he pointed

with accusing finger to the imperturbable Bristow.

"That man there," he declared, a crawling contempt in his voice, "is the thief and the murderer!"

For a heavy moment the incredible accusation stunned the entire group.

"Mr. Braceway," said Bristow, looking now at Fulton and Greenleaf, "is suffering a delusion."

The two men, however, afforded him no support. They kept their eyes on Braceway. They gave the effect of falling away from some evil contagion.

"Because," Bristow continued, "I have been the innocent victim of trumped up charges of embezzlement by the crookedest man in a crooked business, he accuses me of murder when——"

"Shut up!" commanded Braceway, dropping his hand to his side.

He flashed the pawn broker a quick glance.

Abrahamson leaned over and rapped with his knuckles on the door to the porch. It opened, admitting two policemen in uniform.

"I took the liberty, chief," Braceway apologized, "of requesting them to be here. I knew you'd want them to do the right thing, and promptly."

Greenleaf gulped, nodded acquiescence. Stunned as he was, the detective's manner forced him into believing the charge.

Bristow's smile had faded. But, save for a pallor that wiped from his checks their usual flush, there was no evidence of the conflict within him. So far as any notice from him went, the policemen did not exist.

One of them stepped forward and laid a hand on his shoulder.

He ignored it.

"Perhaps," he said, sarcasm in his voice, his eyes again on Braceway, "it will occur to you that I've a right to know why this outrage is committed."

Once more he commanded Greenleaf with his eyes.

"The chief of police will hardly sanction it without some excuse, without a shadow of evidence."

"Yes," Greenleaf complied waveringly. "Er—that is—er—I suppose you're certain about this, Mr. Braceway?"

"Let's have it! Let's have it all!" demanded Fulton, articulate at last, his clenched hands shaken by the palsy of rage.

Bristow, with a careless motion, brushed away the policeman's hand.

"By all means," he said, imperturbable still; "I demand it. I'm not guilty of murder. Not by the wildest flight of the craziest fancy can any such charge be substantiated."

Greenleaf, noting his iron nerve, his freedom from the slightest sign of panic, was dumbfounded, and believed in his innocence again.

"I have the proofs," Braceway said to the chief. "Do you want them here, and now?"

"It might be—er—as well, and—and fair, you know. Yes."

Abrahamson swung the porch door shut. The two policemen stood back of Bristow's chair. Greenleaf, still bewildered, laid a calming hand on

Fulton's shoulder. The old man was shaking like a leaf.

"All right," agreed Braceway. "I can give you the important points in a very few minutes; the high lights."

CHAPTER XXVIII

CONFESSION VOLUNTARY

BRACEWAY leaned against the mantel, relaxed, swinging his cane slowly in his right hand, a careless, easy grace in his attitude. He addressed himself to Fulton and Greenleaf, an occasional glance including Abrahamson in the circle of those for whose benefit he spoke.

Bristow listened now in unfeigned absorption, estimating every statement, weighing each detail. The tenseness of his pale face showed how he forced his brain to concentration.

"Having decided that the bearded man and the murderer were the same," Braceway began, "I asked myself this question: 'Who, of all those in Furmville, is so connected with the case now that I am warranted in thinking he did the previous blackmailing and this murder?' And I eliminated in my own mind everybody but Lawrence Bristow. He was the one, the only one, who could have annoyed Mrs. Withers one and four years ago, respectively, and also could have murdered her.

"Morley was at once out of the reckoning; he had known the Fultons for only the past three years. To consider the negro, Perry Carpenter, would have been absurd. Withers, of course, was beyond suspicion. Everything pointed to Bristow.

"With that decision last Wednesday afternoon, I went to Number Five and got all the finger-prints visible on the polished surfaces of the chair which was handled, overturned, in the living room the night of the murder. Fortunately, this polish was inferior enough to have been made gummy by the rain and dampness that night; and, in the stress of the few days following, had been neither dusted nor wiped off.

"Bristow did not touch this chair the morning the murder was discovered. In fact, he cautioned everybody not to touch it.

"Reliable witnesses say he didn't touch it between then and the time I got the finger-prints. He declares he was never in the bungalow before he entered it in response to Miss Fulton's cry for help.

"I found on the chair the finger-prints of five different persons, four afterwards identified: Miss Fulton, the coroner, Miss Kelly and Lucy Thomas. The fifth I was unable to check up then.

"I did so later, in Washington.

"It was identical with the print of Bristow's fingers on the glass top of a table in his hotel room there. I didn't depend on my own judgment for that. I had with me an expert on finger-prints. And finger-prints, as you all know, never lie.

"All this established the fact, beyond question, that Bristow had been secretly in the living room of Number Five before, or at the time of, the commission of the crime."

He paused, giving them time to appreciate the full import of that chain of facts.

For the space of half a minute, the room was a study in still life. The sound of Fulton's grating teeth was distinctly audible. Bristow made a quick move, as if to speak, but checked the impulse.

"In Washington," Braceway resumed, "he had the hemorrhage. It was faked—a red-ink hemorrhage. Before the arrival of the physician who was summoned, Bristow had ordered a bellboy to wrap the 'blood-stained' handkerchief and towel in a larger and thicker towel and to have the whole bundle burned at once.

"This, he explained to the boy, was because of his desire that nobody be put in danger of contracting tuberculosis.

"By bribing the porter who had been directed to do the burning, I got a look at both the handkerchief and the towel. They were soaked right enough, thoroughly soaked—in the red ink.

"The physician was easily deceived because, when he came in, all traces of the so-called blood had been obliterated. Altogether, it was a clever trick on Bristow's part.

"His motive for staging it and for arranging for a long and uninterrupted sleep was clear enough. There was something he wanted to do unobserved, something so vital to him that he was willing to take an immense amount of trouble with it. Golson's detective bureau let me have the best trailer, the smoothest 'shadow,' in the business—Tom Ricketts.

"At my direction he followed Bristow from the Willard Hotel to the electric car leaving Washington for Baltimore at one o'clock. Reaching Baltimore at two-thirty, Bristow pawned the emeralds and diamonds at two pawnshops. He caught the four o'clock electric car back to Washington, and was in his room long before six, the hour at which his nurse, Miss Martin, was to wake him.

"On the Baltimore trip he had a left leg as sound as mine and wore no brace of any kind. He did wear a moustache, and bushy eyebrows, which changed his appearance tremendously. Also, he had changed the outline of his face and the shape of his lips.

"While he was in Baltimore, I searched the bedroom in which he was supposed to be asleep.

"Miss Martin, in whom I had been obliged to confide, helped me. We found in the two-inch sole of the left shoe, which of course he did not take with him, a hollow place, a very serviceable receptacle. In it was the bulk of the missing Withers jewelry, the stones unset, pried from their gold and platinum settings.

"They are, I dare say, there now."

The two policemen stared wide-eyed at Bristow. He was, they decided, the "slickest" man they had ever seen.

"You see why he executed the trick? It was to establish forever, beyond the possibility of question, his innocence. Plainly, if an unknown man pawned the Withers jewelry in Baltimore while Bristow slept, exhausted by a major hemorrhage, in Washington, his case was made good, his alibi perfect.

"You can appreciate now how he built up his fake case against Perry Carpenter, his use of the buttons, his creeping about at night, like a villain in cheap melodrama, dropping pieces of the jewelry where they would incriminate the negro most surely, and his exploitation of the 'winning clue,' the finger nail evidence.

"Furthermore, he gave Lucy Thomas a frightful beating to force from her the statement against Perry. In this, he was brutal beyond belief. I saw that same afternoon the marks of his blows on her shoulders. They were sufficient proofs of his capacity for unbridled rage. The sight of them strengthened my conviction that, in a similar mood, he had murdered Mrs. Withers."

"The negro lied!" Bristow broke in at last, his words a little fast despite his surface equanimity. "I subjected her to no ill treatment whatever. Anyway"—he dismissed it with a wave of his hand—"it's a minor detail."

Braceway, without so much as a glance at him, continued:

"And that gave me my knowledge of her being a partial albino. She has patches of white skin across her shoulders, and Perry, in struggling with her for possession of the key to Number Five, had scratched her there badly. That, I think, disposes of the finger nail evidence against Carpenter.

"The rest followed as a matter of course. An examination of Major Ross' collection of circulars describing those 'wanted' by the police of the various cities for the past six years revealed the photograph of Splain. Bristow has changed his appearance somewhat—enough, perhaps, to deceive the casual glance—but the identification was easy.

"I then ran over to New York and got the Splain

story. I knew he was so dead sure of having eluded everybody that he would stay here in Furmville. But, to make it absolutely sure, I sent him yesterday a telegram to keep him assured that I was working with him and ready to share discoveries with him. And I confess it afforded me a little pleasure, the sending of that wire. I was playing a kind of cat-and-mouse game."

Bristow put up his hand, demanding attention. When Braceway ignored the gesture, he leaned back, smiling, derisive.

"Morley's embezzlement and its consequences gave me a happy excuse for keeping on this fellow's trail while he was busy perfecting the machinery for Perry's destruction. The man's self-assurance, his conceit——"

"I've had enough of this!" Bristow cut in violently, exhibiting his first deep emotion. He turned to Greenleaf:

"Haven't you had enough of this drool? What's the man trying to establish anyhow? He talks in one breath about my having changed the outline of my face and the shape of my mouth, and in the next second about recognizing as me a photograph which he admits was taken at least six years ago!

"It's an alibi for himself, an excuse for not being able to prove that I'm the man who pawned the jewelry in Baltimore! It's thinner than air!"

But Greenleaf's defection was now complete.

"Go on," he said to Braceway. The more he thought of the full extent to which the embezzler had gulled him for the past week, the more he raged.

"Not for me! I don't want any more of the drivel!" Bristow objected again, his voice raucous and still directed to Greenleaf. "What's *your* idea? I admit I'm wanted in New York on a trumped-up charge of embezzlement. This detective, by a stroke of blind luck, ran into that; and, as I say, I admit it.

"You can deal with that as you see fit; that is, if you want to deal with it after what I've done for law and order, and for you, in this murder case.

"But you can't be crazy enough to take any stock in this nonsense about my having been connected with the crime. Exercise your own intelligence! Great God, man! Do you mean to say you're going to let him cram this into you?"

He got himself more in hand.

"Think a minute. You know me well, chief. And you, Mr. Fulton, you're no child to be bamboozled and turned into a laughing stock by a detective who finds himself without a case—a pseudo expert on crime who tries to work the age-old trick of railroading a man guilty of a less offense!"

"This is no place for an argument of the case," Braceway said crisply. "Mr. Abrahamson, tell us what you know about this man."

"It is not much, Mr. Braceway," the Jew replied; "not as much as I would like. I've seen him several times; once in my place when he was fixed up with moustache and so forth, and twice when he was fixed up with a beard and a gold tooth; once again when he was sitting out here on his porch."

Abrahamson talked rapidly, punctuating his phrases with quick gestures, enjoying the importance of his rôle.

"Mr. Braceway," he explained smilingly to Greenleaf, "talked to me about the man with the beard—talked more than you did, chief. You know Mr. Braceway—how quick he is. He talked and asked me to try to remember where and when I had seen this Mr. Bristow. I had my ideas and my association of ideas. I remembered—remembered hard. That afternoon I took a holiday—I don't take many of those—and I walked past here. 'I bet you,' I said to myself—not out real loud, you understand—'I bet you I know that man.' And I won my bet. I did know him.

"This Mr. Splain and the man with the beard are the same, exactly the same."

Bristow's smile was tolerant, as if he dealt with a child. But Fulton, his angry eyes boring into the accused man, saw that, for the first time, there were tired lines tugging the corners of his mouth. It was an expression that heralded defeat, the first faint shadow of despair.

"You have my story, and I've the facts to prove it a hundred times over," Braceway announced. "Why waste more time?"

"For the simple reason," Bristow fought on, "that I'm entitled to a fair deal, an honest——"

On the word "honest" Braceway turned with his electric quickness to Greenleaf, and, as he did so, Bristow leaned back in his chair, as if determined not to argue further. His face assumed its hard, bleak calm; his cold self-control returned.

"Now, get this!" Braceway's incisive tone whipped Greenleaf to closer attention. "You've an embezzler and murderer in your hands. He admits one crime; I've proved the other. The rest is up to you. Put the irons on him. Throw him into a cell! You'll be proud of it the rest of your life. Here's the warrant."

He drew the paper from his hip pocket and tossed it to the chief.

"Get busy," he insisted. "This man's the worst type of criminal I've ever encountered. Not content with blackmailing and robbing a woman, he murdered her; not satisfied with that, he deliberately planned the death of an innocent man because he, in his cowardice, was afraid to take the ordinary chances of escaping detection. By openly parading his pursuit of breakers of the law, he secured secretly his opportunity to excel their basest actions. He——"

Quicker than thought, Braceway lunged forward with his cane and struck the hand Bristow had lifted swiftly to his throat. The blow sent a pocket knife clattering to the floor. A policeman, picking it up, saw that the opened blade worked on a spring.

The accused man sank back in his chair. The gray immobility of his face had broken up. The features worked curiously, forming themselves for a second to a pattern of mean vindictiveness. His right hand still numbed by the blow, he took his handkerchief with the left and flicked from his neck, close to the ear, a single red bead.

"Search him," Braceway ordered one of the officers.

Bristow submitted to that. When he looked at Braceway, his face was still bleak.

"You've got me," he said in a tone thoroughly matter-of-fact. "I'm through. I'll give you a statement."

"You mean a confession?"

"It amounts to that."

"Not here," Braceway refused curtly. "We've no stenographer."

"I'd prefer to write it myself anyway," he insisted. "It won't take me fifteen minutes on the typewriter." Seeing Braceway hesitate, he added: "You'll get it this way, or not at all. Suit yourself."

The detective did not underestimate the man's stubborn nerve.

"I'm agreeable, chief," he said to Greenleaf, "if you are."

"Yes," the chief agreed. "It's as good here as anywhere else."

Darkness had grown in the room. Abrahamson and the policeman pulled down the window shades. Greenleaf turned on the lights.

Bristow limped to the typewriter and sat down. Braceway opened the drawer of the typewriter stand and saw that it contained nothing but sheets of yellow "copy" paper cut to one-half the size of ordinary letter paper.

Every trace of agitation had left Bristow. Colour crept back into his cheeks.

Braceway and Greenleaf watched him closely. They had the idea that he still contemplated suicide, that he sought to divert their attention from himself by interesting them in what he wrote. They remembered the boast he had made in the cell in New York.

He felt their wariness, and smiled.

CHAPTER XXIX

THE LAST CARD

HE worked with surprising rapidity, tearing from the machine and passing to Braceway each half-page as he finished it. He wrote triple-space, breaking the story into many paragraphs, never hesitating for a choice of words.

"My name is Thomas F. Splain.

"I am forty years old.

"I am 'wanted' in New York for embezzlement.

"Fear is an unknown quantity to me. I have always had ample self-confidence. The world belongs to the impudent.

"I learned long ago that no man is at heart either grateful, or honest, or unselfish."

With a turn of the roller, he flicked that off the machine and, without raising his head, passed it to Braceway. The detective glanced at it long enough to get its meaning and handed it to Fulton. When it was offered to Greenleaf, he shook his head.

The chief's rage had reached its high point. To his realization of how perfectly he had been duped, there was added the humiliation of having two members of his force as witnesses of its revelation.

"If he makes a move," he thought savagely, fingering the revolver in the side pocket of his coat, "I'll kill him certain."

The man at the machine wrote on:

"After leaving New York, I was caught in a street accident in Chicago, suffering a broken nose. Thanks to my physicians—an incompetent lot, these doctors—I emerged with a crooked nose.

"That was a help. I then had all my teeth extracted. Knowing dentistry, I saw the possibilities of disguise by wearing differently shaped sets of teeth.

"Note my heavily protruding lower lip—and, at rare intervals, my hollow cheeks.

"Also, there's your gold-tooth mystery—solved!

"As a disguise, the gold tooth is admirable. I mean a solid, complete tooth of gold, garish in the front part of the mouth.

"It unfailingly changes the expression; frequently, it degrades and brutalizes the face. Try it.

"Using my crooked nose as an every-day precaution, I always straightened it for night work. Forestier taught me that—great man, Forestier; marvellous with noses.

"He is now piling up a fortune as make-up specialist for motion pictures in Los Angeles—has a secret preparation with which he 'builds' new noses.

"Changing the colour of my eyes was something beyond the police imagination.

"I got the trick from a man in Cincinnati—another great character. Homatropine is the basic element of his preparation.

"Some day women will hear of it and make him rich. He deserves it."

Fulton, after he had read that, looked at Braceway out of tortured eyes. This turning of his tragedy into jest defied his strength.

"That's enough of that," Braceway raised his voice above the clatter of the typewriter. "Get down to the crime, or stop!"

"By all means," Bristow assented.

Flicking from the roller the page he had already begun, he tore it up and inserted another.

"I met Enid Fulton six years ago at Hot Springs, Virginia. She fell in love with me.

"I had always known that a rich woman's indiscretions could be made to yield big dividends. She was a victim of her——"

Braceway's grasp caught the writer's hands.

"Eliminate that!" he ordered sternly. "It's not necessary."

Bristow, imperturbable, his motions quick and sure, tore up that page also, and started afresh:

"Later she believed I had embezzled in order to assure her ease and luxury from the date of our marriage.

"Her exaggerated sense of fair play, of obligation, was an aid to my representations of the situation.

"Although she no longer loved me and did love Withers, my hold on her, rather on her purse, could not be broken.

"She gave me the money in Atlantic City and Washington. I played the market, and lost. I no longer had my cunning in dealing with stocks.

"I came here as soon as I had learned of her presence in Furmville. At first, she was reasonable. Abrahamson knows that. I pawned several little things with him.

"At last she grew obstinate. She argued that, if she pawned any more of her jewels, she would be unable to redeem them because her father had failed in business.

"But I had to have funds. Several times I pointed this out to her when I saw her in Number Five—always after midnight, for my own protection as well as hers.

"Finally, my patience was exhausted. Last Monday night, or early Tuesday morning, I told her so, quite clearly.

"She argued, plead with me. All this was in whispers. The necessity of whispering so long irritated me.

"Her refusal, flat and final, to part with the jewels enraged me. It was then that I made the first big mistake of my life.

"I lost my temper. Men who can not control their tempers under the most trying circumstances should let crime alone. They will fail.

"I killed her—a foolish result of the folly of yielding to my rage.

"Standing there and looking at her, I pondered, with all the clarity I could command. In a second, I perceived the advisability of throwing the blame upon some other person."

The faces of Braceway and Fulton mirrored to the others the horror of the stuff they were reading. The scene taxed the emotional balance of all of them. The evil-faced man at the typewriter, the father getting by degrees the description of his daughter's death, the policemen waiting to put the murderer behind bars——

Abrahamson, peculiarly wrought upon by the tenseness of it all, wished he had not come. His back felt creepy. He lit a cigarette, puffed it to a torch and threw it down.

Bristow wrote on:

"Mechanically, my fingers went to a pocket in my vest and played with two metal buttons I had picked up in my kitchen the day before, Monday.

"I knew the buttons had come from the overalls of the negro, Perry Carpenter. It would be easy to drop one there, the other on the floor of my kitchen, where I had originally found them.

"That would be the beginning of identifying him as the murderer. He had been half-drunk the day before.

"The rest was simple—dropping the lavalliere links back of Number Five, placing the lavalliere in the yard of his house, and so on.

"I had one piece of luck which, of course, I did not count on when I first adopted this simple course. That was when Greenleaf asked me to help him in finding the murderer. A confiding soul —your Greenleaf—and insured by nature against brain storms.

"Such a turn was a godsend. I had become the investigator of my own crime.

"There remains to be told only the fact that I made a second trip to Number Five.

"Having come back here in safety, I perceived I had left there without the jewels she was wearing and without those in her jewel cabinet.

"She had brought this cabinet into the living room to show me how her supply of jewelry had been depleted.

"To murder and not get the fruits of it, is like picking one's own pocket. I returned immediately and remedied the mistake.

"Before departing this last time, I switched on the lights to assure myself that I had left only the clue to the negro's presence, none to my own.

"That explains Withers' story of his struggle at the foot of the steps. We really had it.

"In the ordinary course of events, the negro would have gone to the chair.

"But there were complications I did not foresee.

"Morley's theft and clamour for money from Miss Fulton, Withers' jealousy, and my own extra precaution of appearing with beard and gold tooth in the Bernard Hotel, so as to shift suspicion to a mysterious 'unknown' in case of necessity; all these things, with too many clues, presented an embarrassment of riches.

"If I had known of them in advance, either Morley or Withers would have paid the penalty for the crime. The negro would never have received my attention.

"I have no game leg, never have had. The brace made it easy for me to transform myself into a grim, resentful man in my 'private' work.

"I have no tuberculosis, never have had. I have a naturally flat chest. Sluggish veins and capillaries in my face, caused by my having suffer pathological blushing for ten years, cause a permanent flush in my cheeks.

"That was enough to fool the physicians. Besides, when the Galenites have once diagnosed your purse favourably, your disease is what you please.

"I have said my first great mistake was losing my temper with Enid Withers.

"My second was my laughter in the cab the night Braceway and I questioned Morley. I knew he was holding back something, but I never dreamed it was his knowledge of my having done the murder.

"That laugh was suicidal, for it was the disarming of myself by myself.

"But for the albino discovery by Braceway, my conviction would have been impossible. The case against Perry was too strong.

"Still, it is as well this way as another. I should never have served the time for embezzlement. A free life is a fine thing. I suspect that death, perhaps, is even finer."

He handed the last page to Braceway, leaned back in his chair, put up his arms and yawned. The glance with which he swept the faces of those before him was arrogant. It had a sinister audacity.

"The confession's complete," Braceway told Greenleaf, clipping his words short. "Take him away. No—wait!" He pulled a pen from his pocket and turned to the prisoner.

"Oh, the signature," Bristow said coolly. "I forgot that."

He took the typewritten pages roughly from Fulton, and in a bold, free hand wrote at the bottom of each: "Thomas F. Splain."

"I'm ready," he announced, rising from his chair so that he jostled Fulton unnecessarily.

The old man, his self-control broken at last, struck him with open hand full in the face. His fingers left three red stripes across the murderer's white cheek.

Before Braceway could interfere, Bristow checked his impulse to strike back and gave Fulton a long, level look.

"You're welcome to it," he said finally; "welcome, old man. I guess I still owe you something, at that."

"Put the cuffs on him," ordered Greenleaf.

"First, though, I'd like to have a clean collar, some clean linen; and I want to get rid of this brace," Bristow interrupted.

"To hell with what you want!" Greenleaf cried, a shade more purple with rage.

Bristow turned to Braceway:

"You're right. The stuff's in the sole of this shoe."

"Let's take charge of that now," Braceway said to the chief. They each grasped one of the prisoner's arms and hustled him with scant ceremony to his bedroom. Bristow removed his trousers and, unbuckling the belt and straps of the steel brace, took off the thick-soled shoe.

Greenleaf put his hand into it and tugged at the inner sole.

"Opens on the outside," prompted Braceway, "underneath, near the instep."

The chief, after fumbling with it a moment, got it open. The jewels streamed to the floor, a little cascade of radiance and colour. He picked them up, getting down on all-fours so as not to miss one.

"Don't be unreasonable," Bristow complained as he slipped on another shoe. "Let me have a clean shirt and collar."

"Be quick about it," Braceway consented, his voice heavy with contempt.

Greenleaf, holding him again by one arm, shoved him toward the bureau. He got out of his shirt, Greenleaf shifting his grasp so as not to let go of him for a second. In trying to put the front collar button into the fresh shirt, he broke off its head.

"Come on," growled the chief. "You don't need a collar anyway."

"Not so fast! I've more than one collar button."

He put his hand into a tray and picked up another. It had a long shank and was easily manipulated because of the catch that permitted the movement of its head, as if on a hinge.

"This is better," he said, fingering it, unhurried as a man with hours to throw away.

"Get a move on! Get a move!" Greenleaf growled again, tightening his hold until it was painful.

Bristow, apparently bent on throwing off this rough grasp on his left arm, swiftly raised his right hand with the button to his mouth.

For the fraction of a second his eyes, bright and defiant, met Braceway's. The detective, reading the elation in them, shouted:

"Look out!"

There was a click. And Bristow flung away

the button as Braceway caught at his hand.

"I beat you after——" he tried to boast.

But the poison, quicker than he had thought, cut short his utterance. His eyelids flickered twice. He collapsed against Greenleaf and slid, crumpled, to the floor.

"Cyanide," said Braceway. "He had it in the shank of that collar button."

Greenleaf bent over him.

"God, it's quick!" he announced. "He's dead."

THE END

76

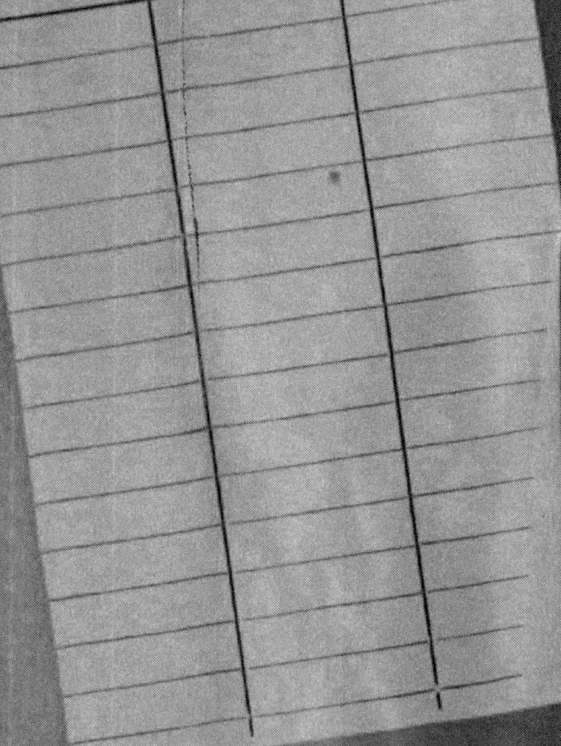

THE NEW YORK PUBLIC LIBRARY
REFERENCE DEPARTMENT

This book is under no circumstances to be taken from the Building

Form 410

www.ingramcontent.com/pod-product-compliance
Lightning Source LLC
Chambersburg PA
CBHW071408050326
40689CB00010B/1792

* 9 7 8 1 1 4 5 9 2 3 9 9 7 *